The Depth
of God's Reach

The Depth
of God's Reach

A Spirituality of Christ's Descent

Michael Downey

ORBIS BOOKS

Maryknoll, New York 10545

ORBIS ✪ BOOKS
Maryknoll, New York 10545

Fathers and Brothers
MARYKNOLL™

Founded in 1970, Orbis Books endeavors to publish works that enlighten the mind, nourish the spirit, and challenge the conscience. The publishing arm of the Maryknoll Fathers and Brothers, Orbis seeks to explore the global dimensions of the Christian faith and mission, to invite dialogue with diverse cultures and religious traditions, and to serve the cause of reconciliation and peace. The books published reflect the views of their authors and do not represent the official position of the Maryknoll Society. To learn more about Maryknoll and Orbis Books, please visit our website at www.maryknollsociety.org.

Library of Congress Cataloging-in-Publication Data

Names: Downey, Michael, author.
Title: The depth of God's reach : a spirituality of God's reach / by Michael Downey.
Description: Maryknoll : Orbis Books, 2018. | Includes bibliographical references.
Identifiers: LCCN 2017036355 (print) | LCCN 2017048274 (ebook) | ISBN 9781608337286 (e-book) | ISBN 9781626982611 (pbk.)
Subjects: LCSH: Jesus Christ—Descent into hell. | Death—Religious aspects—Christianity.
Classification: LCC BT470 (ebook) | LCC BT470 .D69 2018 (print) | DDC 232.96/7—dc23
LC record available at https://lccn.loc.gov/2017036355

Tám
Trong đầm gì đẹp bằng sen
Lá xanh bông trắng lại chen nhị vàng
Nhị vàng, bông trắng, lá xanh
Gần bùn mà chẳng hôi tanh mùi bùn.

Ah, beautiful lotus in the pond,
Yellow pistil in white flower in green leaf,
Green leaf, white flower, yellow pistil,
Fragrance rising up, transcends
the stinking mud.
Tâm

Contents

Introduction

I write on Easter Monday while the echoes of Alleluia ring loudly, as they will continue to do for the fifty days until Pentecost and beyond. It may seem odd that the introduction to a book is written as the writing comes to an end. Perhaps a writer can say what is to be written only after it has been written.

"We are an Easter people and Alleluia is our song." So says, or sings, Saint Augustine! True enough. But how do we sing our song when it is ever so clear that for people and peoples beyond numbering, Christian or other, life today is between cross and resurrection, a time between Good Friday and Easter Sunday? We live in a time of darkness when well-worn and reliable truths ring hollow, when whole worlds of meaning, purpose, and value are dying or dead, when hope seems in short supply. In such a world, choruses of Alleluia are drowned out by the wailing of millions caught in circles of suffering, the silent screaming of the countless living dead in our midst. Speech about God is plausible today only if it reckons with the darkness and death of our terrifying age.

This slim volume has been written from that known-in-the-bones conviction that cheery Christianity will no longer do. Spiritual chumminess has worn out its welcome in a time when it is altogether clear that we are living between the cross and resurrection. No cross, no resurrection. Christian living is always between memory and hope, between promise and fulfillment. Life in Christ is always *toward* Easter. The mystery of Christ's descent is that "moment" of his Pasch when Christ dwelt among the dead bringing light, life, and love to those who seemed beyond hope, in a world, another world, the netherworld beyond God's reach. Because Christ descended among the dead we rest assured, rest in peace, in the knowledge that nothing, that no one, is beyond God's reach.

The ten chapters that follow may be thought of in terms of one writer's effort to sketch out the lyrics of a new song, a song that we must learn to sing from the depths, from the ache of absence, before we dare shout out Easter's Alleluia.

In probing the mystery of Christ's descent among the dead, the work of other theologians who have wrestled with this slippery Christian affirmation has provided me with invaluable insights and the impetus to move forward often amidst the dark patches of reading and writing on this subject over the course of a year and more. Their important work is acknowledged in the way of "Suggestions for Further Reading" at the conclusion of this volume; its placement at the end is in no way indicative of its importance.

At its best, theology is a conversation with friends about the things that really matter. But it can also often be a lonesome task, especially when probing a Christian truth judged to be insignificant, indeed better forgotten, such as Christ's descent among the dead.

It is a cause of deep delight for me to express my thanks to several colleagues who have engaged me in conversation and critique as I have attempted to retrieve the creedal affirmation that Christ descended to the dead from the immense store of what is thought to be theological marginalia. The conversation with each one has challenged me to rethink and rewrite several times in an effort to demonstrate that Christ's descent may, after all, be a most comforting and pastorally useful theological resource with practical implications for the Christian spiritual life.

My first word of thanks goes to Cristóbal Torres, one of the very few to my knowledge who has an abiding theological interest in the mystery of Christ's descent combined with a deep grasp of its implications for the pastoral life of the church. My debt to him is beyond telling.

Peter Cho Phan, no novice in the geography of dying, death, and the afterlife, read this work in an earlier draft and, as on previous occasions, gave of himself generously in an effort to help me clarify my thinking on the subject at hand.

Thomas P. Rausch, colleague and friend over many years, raised serious questions about the value of treating such an obscure and marginal affirmation of the Christian faith. After all, not many theologians throughout the centuries have even thought to wonder about the meaning of Christ's descent among the dead. It has been more of a puzzle than a source for pondering and prayer. Questioning the value of probing the mystery of Christ's descent caused me to redouble my commitment to see this work to completion.

It is a pleasure, indeed an honor, to express my gratitude to one of the few still among us who was and remains witness to the event of the Second Vatican Council. In the spirit of the Council, he welcomed my questions, listened to me deeply, and engaged me in respectful dialogue in search of that which, or the One who, cannot be grasped. It was in conversation with him, the esteemed Ladislas Orsy, that I experienced one of those moments when theology hovers at the edge of prayer.

For his unwavering interest and support of my theological endeavors over more than forty years I express my heartfelt gratitude to Gerard Austin.

As on earlier occasions I here express my thanks for hospitality extended to me by the Trappist monks of l'Abbaye du Mont-des-Cats in Franco-Flanders, and by the Trappistines of Santa Rita Abbey in Arizona's Sonoran Desert. Without the immersion in silence and solitude—dare I say prayer—afforded me by these two monastic communities, the words on these pages would have remained thoughts.

Patrick Markey read the completed manuscript at the eleventh hour, offering an encouraging word and welcome suggestions for improvement.

A final word of thanks to Orbis Books for providing me the opportunity to bring my thoughts to these pages. And to Celine Allen, whose graceful and grace-filled hand touched every page once again.

CHAPTER 1

Speaking of the Dead

I believe in God, the Father almighty,
Creator of heaven and earth,
and in Jesus Christ, his only Son, our Lord,
who was conceived by the Holy Spirit,
born of the Virgin Mary,
suffered under Pontius Pilate,
was crucified, died and was buried;
he descended into hell;
on the third day he rose again from the dead;
he ascended into heaven,
and is seated at the right hand of God
the Father almighty . . .

"HE DESCENDED INTO HELL." Why bother thinking or speaking about this? Why write about death and the dead? And why look to what many think of as a baffling Christian belief to bring light and solace to those who are dying, or to those who are grieving the loss of a loved one, or to those who are overwhelmed by the suffering, dying, and death of millions because of violence, disease, starvation, and systemic injustice? Why focus on a Christian belief often thought to be marginal to the faith to bring hope in the face of dying and death?

Further, why explore the often vexing Christian affirmation that Christ "descended to the dead" or, as some renditions of the Apostles' Creed put it, he "descended into hell"? This latter formulation is the one found in the "new" Roman Missal (2011), while the former is found in the older translation following the reforms of the Second Vatican Council. Are these two different ways of speaking of Christ's descent much of a muchness? Are they roughly approximate terms? Or do they express distinct understandings of Christ's descent?

Why treat the mystery of Christ's descent in a way that is not pitched primarily to scholars, but to spiritual seekers, to pastors and pastoral workers, to students of theology, to anyone seeking a deeper understanding of his or her faith who is willing to stretch a bit in the desire to grow theologically and spiritually? There are three interrelated reasons for doing so.

First, even in what is said to be a secular culture such as ours, there is no lack of interest in death and afterlife. Every human being undergoes death; indeed, everything that lives dies. But we are so reluctant to speak of this universal human reality. I seek to do just that here, in a way that might offer some small reason for the Christian to continue to hope: to hope beyond dying and death.

Some have argued persuasively that entire cultures are built up and sustained by an often unconscious or subconscious denial of death. But inevitably we all must come to terms with the awful truth that being born into this world entails accepting life on life's own terms. And living a human life means accepting suffering, dying, and death as part of the equation. Hard as we might try, there is no escaping this truth.

It meets us at every turn. Death is not singular but plural. There are different kinds and degrees of death. And no one's death is that of another. There are no partners in death. No matter how much support and comfort I may be fortunate enough to receive as I face death, I am alone as I pass from this life.

Death meets us in the passing of a loved one. In the normal course of events it is the passing of a grandparent. And then a parent. There is the passing of a spouse after many years of marriage. Worse, there is the death of a mother's teenage son due to the grip of addiction to heroin. Perhaps worst of all, there is the loss of a child to suicide. These are some of the world-altering, world-shattering events that none of us can escape. Words fail to describe these encounters with death, of being "up close" to death in the passing of another. There is only the ache of an absence that will never be filled. And that anguished cry—sometimes silent, sometimes whispered, often full-throated—that comes from the hollow depths, the very bottom of myself.

In addition to such personal experiences of living up close to deadly suffering and death, there is the abyss of death in which whole groups of peoples—nations, races, and classes—live even while on earth. Dante Alighieri's evocative image of the circles of hell speaks principally to what he maintains awaits some of us after death. But what of the circles of suffering and death in which peoples of warring nations are caught this very day? What of the horror of the living death known by the women who are abducted and held captive, raped before being murdered as a spectacle? What of an entire nation living on edge because of savage attacks on the streets of Paris, by the seaside in Nice, at a little church in a heretofore unknown village in Normandy? Not too far from the north of France is Belgium, a small country deeply wounded by the daily threat of attack. Then there are the nondescript, characterless streets of San Bernardino. And who knows where next? Or who will be next?

When we attend to larger events on the world scene, it is plain that many, indeed most, of us are trapped in the jaws of a devouring death. Millions know nothing of stability—let alone human flourishing—in their struggle to find a way to meet basic human needs in a ravaged and broken world.

How are we to speak of the terrifying times in which we live? What do we call these days, these years in which we live? In times of massive cultural upheaval and widespread social unrest and dismay, care must be taken to avoid trying to manage complexity through descriptive labels such as a "culture of life" as over against a "culture of death." Such designations are of little or no help to so many, entire peoples and cultures caught in the circles of suffering, trapped in a living hell, among the living dead.

And what of the death of systems of meaning, purpose, and value by which generations have lived but are now gone? Deeply held beliefs and moral convictions no longer seem to hold for so many of us. Many live with a profound sense of loss of the big picture. This is often experienced as disruption and disorientation. How to find a way forward amidst the ruins—some of which are of our own making? Amidst the shambles, is there a perch somewhere, some small space of consolation that will allow us to glimpse beyond the terrain of devastation and disintegration?

Apart from all of these deaths we are increasingly mindful of our perishable and perishing planet. Pope Francis's encyclical *Laudato Si': On Caring for Our Common Home* is a summons to attention and action. The earth forever seeks to keep its balance. Everything that lives—from the blade of grass to the caterpillar, to llamas and water buffalos—strives for lasting existence. Of its nature, creation strives, stretches, and groans (Romans 8:22–23). Because of the nature and degree of human interference, the earth cannot keep its balance. It groans. It suffers as it nears extinction. And, following the logic of *Laudato Si'*, it is the poor who suffer the most as a result of the perishing of the earth. This is to say that as human beings driven by unbridled want, gluttony, and greed continue to strangle and suffocate the earth and its resources, we strangle and suffocate the poorest among us.

Overwhelmed by the enormity of suffering and the omnipresence of dying and death—of those dear to us, of whole nations and races and classes of people, of cherished convictions and tightly held beliefs, of our common home Mother Earth— we may, strangely, become distracted from facing the obstinate fact of our own dying and death. And, in addition to being distracted from our own dying and death, in some circumstances we may actually deny the reality that it is coming! In "developed" societies, including the United States, there is a wealthy elite that holds out hope for a kind of immortality through notions of transhumanism or cryogenics or a cyborg future.

Rare indeed is the person who does not fear death. Why are dying and death feared? Because in death we are separated from our own bodies. All that we have experienced, all that we have seen, touched, tasted, heard, and smelled has come to us in and through our body. Loving and being loved is in and through our bodies. What and whom we have known are in and through our bodies; what others have known of us is because of our body. Our delights, our glimpses of beauty, our pleasure and our pain are all possible by virtue of being embodied. What lies ahead once we have been separated from our bodies is unknown to us. And, in the final account, we fear what is unknown, the unknowable.

None of this cancels out the conviction nestled in the believer's heart: I am more than my body. The person I am, the one who knows and is known, the one who loves and is loved, the one who yearns to be free and to set others free, the person I am cannot be reduced to my bodily existence.

This "more" than the body, without which we are not human persons, has been and is called by different names. Throughout Christian history it has often been called the "soul." Sometimes it has been called "spirit." But more than simply the soul, which may be thought of as the life principle or the livingness of everything that lives, human persons are endowed with what might be called a "spiritual soul."

It is the distinctively human capacity for self-transcendence —always stretching and moving beyond our very limited selves by knowing and loving freely—that makes us human persons as such. It is simultaneously the capacity and the exercise of that distinctively human capacity that makes us who we are. And it is this, aptly named the spiritual soul, that is the core of my very self, a core that does not cease to exist when I draw my last breath.

The *second* reason for taking up the topic of this book is to help Christians living in a world seeming to be on the brink of collapse to find resources of hope in the face of dying and death. The reason for Christian hope (1 Peter 3:15) is most often understood in terms of the resurrection of Jesus Christ on the third day. But even as the proclamation that the Crucified One lives has echoed through the centuries, the songs of

Alleluia too often muffle the cruciform configuration of the love of God in Christ. Choruses of Alleluia ring hollow in hearts devastated by loss, by distress, by random violence, by the ravages of mental illness, by the constant threat of terror and destruction. Perhaps it is high time that we shift our gaze to the creedal affirmation that at his death and interment Christ descended among the dead, and here find the surest anchor for Christian life and prayer in our terrifying age.

The descent is the linchpin of Christian faith, for it expresses our conviction that in the darkness in which we are so often enshrouded there is a luminous trace of God's light, life, and love—even there and then—in our dying, in our death, among the dead. The light of Christ has pierced the darkness, has reached so far and so deep as to bring hope to those who are lost and without hope: the dead.

The *third* reason for addressing this thorny topic is to chart out the contours of a spirituality that might sustain those of us living in these days between Friday's suffering and Sunday's glory. In the narrative of Christ's Pasch, on the second day, now called Holy Saturday, nothing happens. Jesus lies in a tomb not his own. In our own time, an age of magnificent distractions beyond counting, our capacity for deep rest and solitude is threatened at every turn. Social media, smartphones, and myriad other devices allow us to be anywhere we want to be, with whomever we want to be, at any time of day or night, anywhere in this world and virtual worlds—diverting our attention from being precisely where we need to be, in our own skin in the here and now and nowhere else with no one else—often a very lonely and solitary place.

Marguerite Duras, one of the outstanding literary figures of twentieth-century France, offers the reminder: "One does not find solitude, one creates it. Solitude is created alone. Solitude is the thing without which one does nothing." The silent waiting before Christ in the tomb is crucial, not only to living meaningfully with the experience of abandonment and oblivion but also as a discipline to cultivate, nurture, and sustain the contemplative emptiness on which spirituality and creative fecundity rest.

The second day, the Saturday called Holy, is the apex of the Christian experience of solitude, of aloneness, of silence. It is the solitude created by faith in hope, a space wherein there is nothing to say, nothing to do, nowhere to go. And where there are no thoughts to be thought. It is known only to those who know how to wait. Perhaps this is the biggest challenge in the spiritual life in our own time and place: waiting. What is to be done is nothing, save waiting on—no, in—the silence of God.

In sum: Why speak of the mystery of Christ's descent, the event between cross and resurrection? The descent of Christ among the dead on Holy Saturday is, on the face of it, a monumental zero, a void. But it is anything but empty, a silence that says everything about God's unfathomable love for those caught in the jaws of death—even those of us mortals dwelling in darkness and the shadow of death. It is here, in the Christian conviction that Christ did truly die, was interred, and descended among the dead that we can discern the stirrings of the Spirit who brings hope in our dark and terrifying age, and that we can perhaps discover the contours of a spirituality rooted in Christ's descent, a way of living in the Spirit who comes in the silence, the emptiness, the solitude, the absence of the second day, in Saturday's waiting.

CHAPTER 2

On Facing into Death

To PASS. Or TO PASS AWAY. This is how many of us were taught to speak of dying and death. My father passed away on July 19, 1990. My grandmother passed on October 9, 1995. In terms more stark, these are the dates on which they died and joined the ranks of all who have died. Whatever one might wish to speculate regarding the whereabouts of their beloved dead in terms of afterlife, that they are among the dead is not a matter for speculation.

Sister M. Regina Loretta, IHM, passed away on January 16, 2012. Of ample girth and contagious laughter, without benefit of a college education, she taught me in the first grade. She was a "boys' nun," teaching elementary school for fifty years or more. For most of those years she taught first-grade boys. Once, after having spent a year teaching in a higher grade, she asked to go back to the "babies" in the first grade.

My last teacher, the distinguished theologian David Noel Power, OMI, passed on June 19, 2014. To provide a list of his publications, his academic appointments, awards, recognitions, and honors would serve no purpose here. By any standards, he was a theological powerhouse throughout his career.

The death of my first teacher and of my last affected me differently. It could perhaps be said that every death affects every person differently. What is common to all is the experience of loss. But what is given to those who put their faith in Jesus Christ is the assurance that our beloved dead are not lost. Each one has found a place before God, with God, in God. This is God's own doing, the One whose name above all naming is Love. And mercy within mercy within mercy.

STRICKEN WITH CANCER while on mission in Zambia, on his return to Washington DC for medical care, David Power was asked by his confreres and friends to reflect on his experience of what he called "facing into death." He named these reflections "Theology in Recline," which later became "Theology in Decline," expressive of his keen awareness of his diminishment and dying as he approached the door of death. The spare humility of his reflections on his own coming death stands out all the more given his stature as a Catholic theologian.

The last of his circular letters to colleagues, confreres, and friends, "On Being Laid Low," opens with lines from the contemporary American poet Mary Oliver's "In Blackwater Woods."

> *Look, the trees*
> *are turning*
> *their own bodies*
> *into pillars*
>
> *of light,*
> *are giving off the rich*
> *fragrance of cinnamon*
> *and fulfillment,*

the long tapers
of cattails
are bursting and floating away over
the blue shoulders

of the ponds,
and every pond,
no matter what its
name is, is

nameless now.
Every year
Everything
I have ever learned

in my lifetime
leads back to this: the fires
and the black river of loss
whose other side

is salvation,
whose meaning
none of us will ever know.
To live in this world

you must be able
to do three things:
to love what is mortal;
to hold it

against your bones knowing
your own life depends on it;
and, when the time comes to let it go,
to let it go.

Toward the end of his life David Power acknowledged that it was a challenge to look into death with no clear understanding of the afterlife. Faith is in a future shown in Christ, but belief about what the future will be like is not clear. David Power continued to return to God's Word and found assurance that God's love endures, without knowing precisely what that might mean in terms of states of being in the afterlife.

His message to those who were with him in prayer or in the hospital during his last few days was expressed in a few unfussy words: "It's part of the passage."

Stripped of everything in those last days in the hospital, David Power was seen clasping a rosary's crucifix. "He wanted to grasp the cross," a faithful woman who stood near him told me later.

Awards, achievements, reputation, accomplishments, notoriety, health, wellbeing—all gone. Only two years after having arrived in Zambia with a one-way ticket in hand, David Power was invited through the door of death in peace, with nothing save the cross of Christ, passaging through the Pasch with the One who forged the passage. And when it came time to let go, he let go.

It is a commonplace to say that forces in contemporary Western culture have contributed to a collective denial of death. There is no point in rehearsing here the evidence of the various ways in which we try to dodge death, finding or creating multiple distractions to avoid facing into death.

SOME ASIAN AND SOUTHEAST ASIAN PEOPLES still manage to cultivate, nurture, and sustain an awareness of death and of those who have died. The celebrated Pulitzer Prize winning Vietnamese-American author Việt Thành Nguyễn reminds Western readers of the presence and power of the ghosts of one's beloved dead, especially those whose lives ended tragically. These do not haunt or frighten. They are not spooks. Their presence reminds those still dwelling on the earth of the enduring bond between the living and those who have died. They teach the living a lesson that throws the saying "You can't take it with you" into reverse. Apparently, there are some things you actually do take with you. All that is unresolved or unhealed, all that binds us and imprisons us on earth is not vanquished at the moment of our death. All is not undone and set right in an instant. In making themselves known to us, our beloved dead serve to remind us that what is bound on earth will be bound beyond death. What is loosed on earth will be loosed beyond.

When visiting my Vietnamese students and my Vietnamese godsons near Little Saigon in Orange County, California, I have found photos of their grandparents and great-grandparents, granduncles and grandaunts dotting their living rooms, the incense sticks always near at hand to venerate those who have gone before them. Ancestor veneration is central to this people, whether they be Buddhist or Catholic, many of the latter finding in that tradition deep resonance with the doctrine of the communion of saints—expressive of the bond between the living and the dead.

It is hard for Westerners to understand the significance of Tết, the Lunar New Year, the only holiday celebrated by everyone in Vietnam regardless of religion. Imagine New Year's Eve, Easter, Memorial Day, July 4th, Labor Day, Thanksgiving, Christmas, and the birthdays of everyone in the family all celebrated in the course of three days—and longer, if possible. Remembrance is at the heart of the festivities. Whether in Little

Saigon in Orange County or in Saigon—now Ho Chi Minh City—people of all ages and from all parts of the world travel great distances for this celebration, flocking to pagodas and churches, gathering at the burial places of their beloved dead. On returning to homes bedecked with pink flowers in the north of Vietnam or yellow flowers in the south, they will place fruits and other favorites of deceased relatives—yes! even a bottle of brandy or a pack of cigarettes—on a small altar before their photos in the living room. Unlike the Western practice of discarding jack-o'-lanterns and Christmas trees immediately after the holidays, in this celebration the photos of the beloved dead are not taken down but continue to be reverenced throughout the year. Apart from Tết, families celebrate the hundred days after the passing of their beloved dead and pay them homage through annual celebrations of their deaths.

ONE OF MY EARLIEST MEMORIES is that of being brought by my grandmother to the wake of an old bachelor from a village near our "home place." We walked the distance in the dark— no cars, no tar, only a narrow gravel path in those hills of Donegal. The old bachelor's yellowed body was laid out in a plain wooden casket in the middle of the front room of the house. People sat for a long while on stiff, wooden, straight-backed chairs in a big circle in the big room. At the center was the corpse of the dead man. The old folks whispered their prayers in Irish. They chatted quietly with one another, alternating between Irish and English—a litany of the poor old bachelor's virtues and vices, one of which was the Irish curse, "the drink." Little wonder his body was yellow!

Small glasses of whiskey were poured. Then the keening pierced the room—those screeching old white-haired women draped in black shawls, half their teeth gone or rotten in their heads, whose job it was to wail at the loss of the bachelor who had no one but them to lament his passing. The sights and sounds and smell and touch of death soaked and saturated the room, right down into the earthen floor on which my grandmother and I knelt when it came our turn to pay respects to the dead bachelor. Amidst the jangling of the rosaries with the Hail Marys rattled off in Irish in the wide circle of that big room my grandmother whispered to me: "The auld boy's body is there in the box you're seein'. But surely to God his soul is somewhere between heaven and here."

Even though I had had earlier intuitions, from that moment until now I have sensed that there is movement, action, perhaps even progress after we draw our last breath. But that is God's doing. Death is not the end. And whatever lies beyond, or follows after, death is not static.

ON ONE OF THOSE SIGNATURE SUNNY AFTERNOONS in Los Angeles, while I was having lunch with a colleague, he expressed interest in the topic of this volume. A man of deep Catholic faith and sharp theological acumen, he does not, however, see much merit in speaking of what might be called an intermediate state or states after death. In his view—sometimes referred to as "resurrection in death"—at our death we are brought into new life with the Risen Lord. Or not. God raises the just to life, but not the damned. For the damned, death is the end. It is not a matter of the damned being condemned for all eternity; rather, it is that they simply cease to exist. Full stop! Reflection, then, on such notions as purgatory, or the difference between the particular judgment and the general judgment, or the relationship between the judgment at the moment of our death and a final judgment, is rather pointless, because it is beyond us to know about these things with any measure of certitude. And so we are left with a final breath and a thumbs up (in dying, the person is with the Lord) or a thumbs down (in dying, the person does not exist).

There is a kernel of truth here that gives reason for hesitation in speaking about what happens at our death and after, because human beings are bound by time and space. We live at a particular period of history in a specific location, or locations. Our days are numbered. As the psalmist puts it, we have "seventy years or eighty for those who are strong" (Psalm 90:10). In whatever is said about what lies beyond our death, caution must be taken lest we think that the categories of space and time apply. What awaits us beyond death is not bound by human categories of time and space.

Be that as it may, because we are creatures in time and space, if we are to speak of what lies beyond the grave, we *cannot not* use categories of time and space. Our efforts to speak meaningfully of what Catholic theology calls "the last things" are part of what Peter Phan calls the eschatological imagination. Thus we speak of heaven, hell, and purgatory as places. But they are not. And we think of eternity as a never-ending succession of days. But it is not. All our efforts to speak or think of what happens after death produce not certitudes but "approximations," that is to say, they are not literal descriptions of the afterlife. It may be helpful here to think of time and space as one universe, while what lies beyond the grave is a different universe that is altogether and entirely different from what we can know and say of the universe we mortals now inhabit.

Indeed, there is no certain knowledge about what happens at our death, or after. But in the same way that we draw on image and story to convey fundamental beliefs of the Christian faith—such as the resurrection of the Crucified One and our own bodily resurrection—so too all we have at hand is the richness of imagination—art, poetry, literature, narrative, and music—to steer clear of literalistic assertions about what happens after death, while at the same time being lured into this mystery through faltering attempts to speak of it rightly in roughly approximate terms.

Recognizing the limits of speaking about what happens at death and in its aftermath, so much in the Christian tradition suggests that there is more than thumbs up or thumbs down as we draw our last breath. Might it be that what awaits us is something akin to life as we know it? Is it possible that after death there is activity, movement, growth, even the possibility of change? Or are death and its aftermath static, final, the end? The weight of the Catholic tradition inclines in the direction of the former. The very notion of purgatory suggests that most of us are not altogether and entirely at the end of the journey, the passage, when we draw our last breath.

"Between heaven and here." My grandmother's words captured the imagination of a boy on his aching knees at prayer before a yellowing, black hooded corpse. It is the imagination, the story, the painting, the poem that gives hints. The rational, logical, modern mind that wants proof and verification of exactly what will happen in any situation here or beyond is frustrated, indeed vexed, in the face of death. But the deepest and most important things—love, beauty, delight, suffering, diminishment, and death—cannot be captured in concept, idea, or even words.

Recognizing the limits of the language of "place," or "state," or "condition," these terms are part of the Christian eschatological imagination by which we seek to describe however inadequately the Christian's future, indeed the future of Christians. Our beloved dead, as well as those dead who are long forgotten, are not lost. And those who are and have been lost may be found because of the generous descent of the Crucified One unto death, among the dead. He shares the lot of those forgotten who lie in the darkness of the netherworld. There is no place, no space, no circumstance or condition beyond the reach of God's love and mercy. Christ's self-emptying love by which he descends to the dead, or into hell, makes the terrain beyond all hope a precinct of epiphany.

CHAPTER 3

Continuing *Kenosis*

IN THE ENCYCLICAL *FIDES ET RATIO*, John Paul II calls attention to the importance of the *kenosis*, the self-emptying of God in Christ, for probing the mystery of God (92–99). He writes: "The very heart of theological inquiry will thus be the contemplation of the mystery of the Triune God" (93). Further, "From this vantage point, the prime commitment of theology is seen to be the understanding of God's *kenosis*, a grand and mysterious truth for the human mind, which finds it inconceivable that suffering and death can express a love which gives itself and seeks nothing in return" (93). All this is in line with Hans Urs von Balthasar—whose theology of *kenosis*, descent, and Holy Saturday underpins this present volume.

Von Balthasar's principal interest, best articulated in his *Mysterium Paschale*, is located in an unusual place: the mystery of Christ's descent into hell, which he understands as the center of all Christology. Because the descent is the final point reached by the *kenosis*, the consummate expression of the love of the Triune God, the Christ of Holy Saturday is the icon par excellence of what God is like. For von Balthasar, the crucifixion of Jesus of Nazareth is not a prelude. But he understands the One who was raised on Easter morn not so much as the

Crucified, but as the One who for us went down among the dead, into hell.

Von Balthasar's view is in sharp contrast to nearly all traditional accounts of Christ's descent as a triumphant, victorious preaching to the just, and only the just, who have come before Christ. Von Balthasar stresses Christ's solidarity with the dead, his finding himself in a situation of complete estrangement and alienation from the Father. For von Balthasar, the descent demonstrates the costliness of redemption: the Son underwent the event of godlessness. Still more: the descent demonstrates that the God revealed in the Son is a Trinity. Through the Spirit as bond of love between the Father and the Son, the relationship of Father and Son is not severed in their estrangement in the descent. The unity of the Father and Son is maintained. In the final humiliation of the One who is Suffering Servant and Son, the glory of God is supremely revealed from the deepest reaches of self-giving love.

It is for this reason that John Paul II suggests that the self-emptying of God in Christ, the divine self-abandon, is the point of entry into the Christian mystery in our own time and place.

While *Fides et Ratio* is of interest principally to theologians and philosophers, *kenosis* may be understood as key to understanding every other Christian mystery, indeed each dimension of Christian faith and practice. This is because in the Christian dispensation, the human relationship with God is made possible by the One who is invisible, intangible, and inaudible becoming one of us in the person of Jesus Christ so that the love of God beyond all naming can be seen, touched, and heard.

As mentioned earlier, understanding our relationship with God in spatial terms has real limits. God is Unfathomable

Mystery well beyond the categories of space and time. Nonetheless, we speak of heaven as "up" and hell "below." Purgatory is somewhere in between. God is thought to be up in heaven and we mortals on earth down below. Even with its limitations, working within such a spatial framework allows us to say that in the quest for God we must begin with the pouring forth of God's love on the earth in Jesus Christ who, as the Son and Word of the Father, is the love of God speaking in a fleshly way. Beholding the lowliness of God in the crib at Bethlehem, we may be led to the fullness of the divine life. We move from bottom to top, from down below to up above, from *kenosis* to the mystery of the Divine Trinity, the Three in One Love, named Father, Son, and Spirit.

The Trinity is the central mystery of Christian faith and life (*Catechism of the Catholic Church*, 234). But if the Trinity remains obscured by thick layers of metaphysical concepts such as three persons of one substance, how are we to understand all the other dimensions of Christian faith and practice? We do so not by imagining God as three people up in the heavens living in a sort of self-imposed blissful solitary confinement. Rather we begin low, with the love that is poured out on the face—into the very soil—of the earth through the Incarnation of God in Christ.

Often thought to be a single event in time and space when the Father's Son and Word comes "down" and is born in Bethlehem, the *kenosis* is better understood as the pattern of Jesus' entire life, ministry, passion, dying, death, and descent. According to some of the Fathers of the Syriac churches, such as Isaac, Ephraim, Aphrahat, and Jacob of Sarug, the mystery of the *kenosis* begins with creation and is manifest not only in the Incarnation but also in a succession of descents in the life of Christ.

To speak of the *kenosis* is indeed to speak of the Incarnation of God in Christ. This is nothing more, or less, than the mystery of Christ's identification with the human reality, the *first* moment or movement of the *kenosis*, of self-emptying, best understood in light of Philippians 2:6–8:

> Christ Jesus, though he was in the form of God,
> did not regard equality with God
> something to be grasped.
> Rather, he *emptied himself*,
> taking the form of a slave,
> coming in human likeness;
> and found human in appearance,
> he humbled himself,
> becoming obedient to the point of death,
> even death on a cross.

Although there are other scriptural accounts wherein we hear and learn of the limits of human efforts and systems of thought in contrast to the folly of wisdom crucified on the cross, what is commonly called the Philippians Hymn provides the surest foundation for an understanding of God's *kenosis*.

Jesus called Son reveals to us God's fatherhood offered to the world as a gift made known in Christ's presence on earth. God is seen, touched, and heard in Jesus, Son and Word of the Father. From the vantage point of *kenosis*, God comes without pretension, in contrast to the hubris of us mortals. The *kenosis* puts a bold question mark in front of our effort to figure it all out so that we can be in control of our life and destiny. The *kenosis* challenges our lofty thoughts and sometimes our most noble activities. The divine mystery does not rest in God's inscrutability—that God's ways are above the ways of mortals—but in that God should appear on the earth in such a fashion, altogether vulnerable and powerless. God does not enter the world at our beck and call like a Hollywood superhero who makes things different because of our prayers—no matter how fervent. The mystery of *kenosis* suggests that God's healing presence is known in the manner of accompaniment. Emmanuel, God with us, is present even and especially amidst the pain and suffering that are part of being mortal. When suffering and darkness do not lift, it is only faith, hope, and love that can endure their weight. Indeed there are times when God's presence is known in the healing of the body, the lifting of the spirit, the visitation of light in the darkest night. These we may anticipate, even though we cannot know how and why God brings healing and relief in some cases and not in others. Such visible and tangible manifestations of God's nearness in human life, in history, in the world, and in the church provide occasion for thanksgiving among those who have sowed in tears but now reap rejoicing— especially if these manifestations are recognized as signs of God's kingdom among us, making visible God's continuing presence in the work of salvation.

Kenosis is the manner in which God appears, refusing to identify with human achievement, resisting the inordinate need, or demand, to measure success and bask in our grand achievements. All these defy the language and the logic of the gift of God, the emptying out of Love itself in order to appear on the scene of human weakness and vulnerability, so as to identify with human beings in the concrete circumstances of their lives. This is a God who does not fill in for human want, serving as a last resort when all else fails, but who is present *amidst* our powerlessness and vulnerability, *amidst* human longing and want. This is the meaning of God's *kenosis*. And the most important practical lesson for discipleship today is this: We must give up a naïve view of a very active God, intervening, filling in the gaps where our minds and efforts fail. In so doing, we consent to the *kenosis*, not only of God in Christ, but in our own living and in the lives of others.

It is common to still find residues of the heretical impulse that the early Church Fathers sought to eradicate: that in the person of Jesus Christ there is only one, divine nature; that Christ's body was not human, and so his sufferings were apparent but not real.

Once we consent to the *kenosis* we too may be cast aside, indeed pushed outside the bounds of respectable society, shoved to the edge of religious systems, like the infant at Bethlehem. We may find ourselves at the edges of the church, pushed to the brink with the crucified teacher and minister of mercy outside the city walls on Golgotha. *Kenosis* calls not only for a way of discipleship in which we are to be compassionate with Christ broken and spent on the cross. Just as much, it demands a commitment to solidarity with all those who have been pushed and shoved to the edges of a society and a church that render so many voiceless, useless, a nuisance. Consenting to *kenosis* may entail being nailed alongside others who are victims of destruction and dehumanization, finding oneself on the outside, even while living at the heart of the church. Following Jesus on the way to the Father through the gift of the Spirit, God's very life within us, may require that "liminality"—living faith at the edge, even and especially at the edge of the church—be embraced as a permanent factor of our existence.

Marginality was not a phase of Jesus' life and ministry. Jesus was, in a description now well known through the work of scripture scholar John Meier, a marginal Jew.

Living in such a place long enough we come to see that the edges may be the center. It is in the depths of our own experience of those marginalized and peripheral dimensions of ourselves, those painful memories that we have pushed and shoved from our consciousness, that we may come to know that God is the God of self-emptying, the One whose very life is Love pouring itself forth. It is there too that our own limits are known above all in our inability to comprehend the magnitude of God's love in Christ who suffers with us and for us and expects nothing in return.

The infant at Bethlehem grows in age and wisdom. In anticipation of his public ministry, Jesus goes to the River Jordan to be baptized by John. He is not sprinkled with water on the forehead as is, lamentably, the practice in so many churches today. Most Roman Catholic practices of baptism — particularly of infant baptism, in which a few drops of water trickle down the forehead of the newborn — take away the strength of the symbolism of immersion into the dying and rising of Christ, and make of a bold symbol a weak one. Rather, in the *second* movement of continuing *kenosis*, Jesus goes down into the water and is plunged into its depths.

It is in the waters of the Jordan that Jesus may be said to take on the sins of the world. Water is not only cleansing, refreshing, and purifying. It is also the dwelling place of devouring and destructive forces often depicted as water dragons and monstrous flesh-eating creatures of the sea. Water is life, but it can also be frightening and life-threatening. By going down into the Jordan, Jesus confronts the forces of evil, so that water can purify and sanctify those who go down into the waters of baptism.

Contemplating the mystery of Christ, we must attend to the whole narrative span that includes, first, the proclamation of the kingdom for which he has been sent in the power of the Spirit; then, his testimony to the Father and his kingdom before the "powers"; and finally, his surrender of himself to the Father on the cross, the one for the many. But before setting out on that road of downward mobility that leads to Calvary, Jesus must undergo a third movement of *kenosis*, an emptying out of himself before the powers of evil.

The narrative of the days in the wilderness in the Gospel of Matthew is to be read together with the account of the baptism of Jesus at the hands of John the Baptist. The astounding experience that Jesus had at the Jordan, the Father's answer to his quest for the kingdom, and the sense of mission that went with it, required that he withdraw a while to ponder what it all meant and to pray about what it might mean for his own proclamation of the coming of the kingdom.

Upon his anointing by the Spirit, Jesus *was driven out* into the wilderness. The sense of God and God's kingdom that had been given to him was so amazing, so initially preposterous from a Jewish perspective, that a period of retreat into the desert was necessary. He had to wrestle with this truth, a matter that is nicely if briefly put by Mark who says that Jesus spent his time there among wild beasts and was ministered to by angels.

This is a contrast story, one that contrasts with the story of the first man, Adam, in the Garden of Eden. There God had walked in the cool of the evening, in a place where humans and animals lived in harmony, and where sin would introduce disorder, conflict, and estrangement. In the wilderness Jesus restores the peaceable kingdom (Isaiah 11:1–9); he is with the wild animals suffering no harm. The angels who once blocked the path of the sinner Adam to the tree of life (Genesis 3: 24) now minister to Jesus, the new Adam, bringing him some small comfort.

The other gospels—Matthew (4:1–11) and Luke (4: 1–13)—describe Jesus' discernment in more elaborate terms. What is it to live only by God's Word, with fidelity matching fidelity? What is it to reject the power of domination and possession and to know no power other than that of service to the kingdom and the proclamation of the Word? What is it to work within the temporal while serving the priority of the spiritual, yet healing the temporal and, even more specifically, those who are badly tempered by greed, lust, anger, envy, mental illness, and possession of all sorts? What is the true nature of trusting the Father's fidelity in the midst of tribulation and to do God's will in service of the kingdom?

All the testing is attributed to Satan, and Matthew and Luke give us a dramatized version of Jesus' conversion to the truth of the kingdom from sincere but simple fidelity to the Law. Jesus and Satan are the characters in the play, but God's presence on the scene is always put to the fore by Jesus. What Satan puts to the fore is the work of the spirits that inject their influence into every human life even and, especially insidiously, into the hearts of those who trust in God and put their lives at the service of God and the spread of the good news.

Commonly known as the temptations of Jesus in the desert, these can also be understood as a *third* moment or movement of the *kenosis*, in which he stands empty, physically and spiritually, so as to be filled with the fullness of the God he calls Abba.

Jesus knew the physical hunger, as well as the spiritual and mental pain of the people of Galilee. He believed that in God's covenant, the people's pain should be alleviated. The wilderness in which Jesus spent this time was not a desert of silky white sands but a barren place of gray soil, littered with small, sometimes jagged, stones. If only these stones were crusty loaves of bread! Jesus could take a shortcut and relieve not only his own hunger but that of the people by changing the stones into loaves of bread. But Jesus draws the Father into the scene by reminding Satan that in the kingdom, the first and most basic thing to do is to listen to the Word of God and to discern the work of God in drawing all people to himself.

The Jewish people at this time were under foreign occupation. In Galilee they were the victims of the self-indulgence and reckless waste of the puppet king, Herod. They had all heard of the reign of God but they knew only the reign of Caesar and the reign of the Herodians. From these they desperately wanted release. Satan in his own ways—battle, revolt, deceit, fraud, infiltration—could provide a means of liberation. All Jesus had to do was to accept this dominion and set out to preach these as means of gaining some freedom. However, again invoking the Father's presence in the conversation, he withdrew from these insinuations and pledged fidelity to the way the Father would show to freedom of spirit, to compassion with the suffering, to fidelity to the Torah, leaving the consequences of conversion to these ways to God and God alone.

Finally, Satan suggested that there was at least one sure way in which Jesus could make his presence felt and gather an immediate following. He could do something spectacular, something grand, such as throwing himself down from the pinnacle of the temple in the heart of Jerusalem, proving that he was indeed God's prophet being looked after by angels. But Jesus opted for the more patient and indeed long-suffering way of preaching God's Word, of calling others to covenant fidelity, and of showing his power through works of genuine service and abundant compassion.

The forty days were thus a time when Jesus drew near to the Father, opened himself to the inspiration of the Spirit, and pondered his choices. How all of this would eventually work out Jesus did not know. In the wilderness he did come to a knowledge of the road on which he was to set out, the journey on which he was to embark.

As an old saying for the Stations of the Cross used to have it, we can "compassionate him" in his choices, knowing that they had to be made over and over again in what lay ahead of him, and ask that we might understand this revelation as it is given to us when faced with often quite gnarly choices in our own lives here and now.

Surely we all know something of the thrilling but devastating nature of the questions Satan puts to Jesus, as well as the many others put to each one of us personally. From the perspective of Christian faith and spirituality, these are tests—indeed temptations—that we all must undergo. Each one of us is to enter into the depths of the heart by entering into the heart of Jesus, reflecting on our own choices which, by the gift of the Spirit, are to be made in the light of those of Jesus. In so doing we are plunged more deeply into the mystery of being called and being in truth children of God, learning to let our lives be enlightened and rendered joyful in the Father's love shown in the baptism of the Lord and in the wilderness, as well as in our own baptism and in all our own decisions and actions throughout the course of our lives.

But then each one of us faces our own particular tests and trials. These we must all ponder, not only when we have the opportunity for periods of quiet reflection or retreat from our very busy lives but even and especially in the midst of them. The first step here is to consent to our own *kenosis*, emptying and then opening ourselves to the gift of the Spirit, more powerful than any spirits, good or bad, that may have sway over us. And then to learn with him that, amidst our own confrontations with the "powers," what matters in the end is fidelity to God alone, our fidelity longing to match God's own fidelity.

Having been emptied entirely in the wilderness Jesus begins his public ministry, during the entire course of which he bends low to be with the lowly, those who are considered to be the dregs of decent society, the dust of the earth. He preaches and teaches earthy mortals, reaching down to those at the very edges of religious and socio-political structures. In the mind's eye we can see him bending down to look into the eyes of the woman bent double (Luke 13:10–17), she who was longing for healing but could not stand upright and ask him face to face. Perhaps on bended knee, Jesus looks into the eyes of the child as he urges his disciples to become little, close to the ground, like a child. It is likely that he bent down to put his finger in the dust to write the only words the gospel depicts him writing. It is hard to imagine him healing the daughter of

Jairus without bending down to her in her sickbed, or doing the same when healing the mother-in-law of Peter.

The Gospel of John tells of Jesus washing the feet of his disciples (13:1–15). At the completion of this task he instructs his disciples to do unto others "as I have done for you." In catechesis and in preaching on the narrative of the foot washing, all attention is given to the service rendered by Jesus in washing the feet of others. Little or no attention is given to the self-emptying, the generous descent, the divine condescension made manifest in Jesus bending down low to the lowest and most unsightly part of the disciples' bodies—their filthy feet!

These are just a few of the gospel images of Jesus' downward movement to the lowest of places and people.

While all the details of the Stations of the Cross do not find mention in the gospel narratives of Jesus on the way to his death, the longstanding prayerful practice of making the Stations, the Via Dolorosa, allows the Christian to touch more deeply a *fourth* movement of this ongoing *kenosis* of Jesus. During what might seem like long pauses in the movement from his condemnation to his entombment, Jesus falls to the ground: down once, down twice, down three times.

After the first fall, Jesus picks himself up and continues to carry his cross, even as he is aware that he is moving slowly and painfully toward Calvary. Down, flat on his face, sweaty grime thick in his beard and hair, he somehow finds the strength to rise from the second fall. He carries on. Then there is the third fall. He is down. And from here he cannot pick himself up and move forward. There is no strength left. He is spent. Exhausted in spirit, depleted of energy, he is ground into the dust of the earth. Indeed he is the dust of the earth—insignificant, bothersome, dirt. Not able to budge, he is turned over entirely into the hands of those who are to put him to death. But they do not do so until they strip him of his clothing. Utterly humiliated, naked before the jeering crowd, he is ridiculed and mocked as his mortal flesh is ripped and torn, as his hands and feet are nailed to the cross, as he hangs gasping for breath, his flesh lanced open as he strains to look upward to the Father.

In the *fifth* movement of ongoing *kenosis*, in his dying and death on the cross, Jesus himself is the very seed about which he had preached to his disciples: Unless a grain of wheat falls to the ground, down into the earth, and dies, it remains a single grain. But if it dies, it will bear much fruit. (John 12:24).

Because Jesus has no place of his own in which to be buried, his body is taken down from the cross and set down in a tomb donated by the disciple Joseph of Arimathea. Is this the terminus of the *kenosis*?

With his death and his interment, Jesus' way of downward mobility has most certainly reached its end. Or has it? The kenotic humiliation, rather than ending with the death and interment of Christ, continues and is extended in the descent among the dead.

The kenotic pattern of the life and mission of Jesus is extended and completed as he goes lower still, descends farther still. The one who comes down to meet us, bringing God's generous love in the Incarnation, baptism, temptation in the wilderness, passion, and cross, goes down lower still, even into the regions of death. He is lowered into a tomb and goes down farther still in order to reach those in utter darkness. This mystery of faith, that Christ "descended into hell" or, more accurately, descended to the dead, continues and completes the pattern of Christ "going down," going lower and lower to meet us in our human condition, going so far as to die as one of us, with us and for us. The reconciliation of the world was brought about through a complete identification by God with suffering humanity, dying humanity, dead humanity— even those who are thought to be beyond all hope in the clutches of hell. In the descent, God's power is seen as that which comes all the way down in suffering love to the nadir of human depravity, debauchery, estrangement, and alienation to bring forth life. In the language and logic of gift, in the descent among the dead the *kenosis* is brought to conclusion.

Following the lead of the French philosopher Paul Ricoeur, biblical scholar Walter Brueggemann has developed an intriguing way of understanding the psalms and bringing them to bear on the spiritual life. In his *Praying the Psalms* Brueggemann suggests that the psalms bespeak basic movements in human life: orientation, disorientation, reorientation.

There is the movement from stability to instability, from a sense of wellbeing into the "pit." This happens when our world collapses around us and we feel that there is no way out of the deep hole into which we have sunk. Then there is the movement out of the pit to a new understanding of ourselves, others, the world, and God. We suddenly understand what has happened and who has brought us up out of the pit. Are not all our lives a movement from order to disorder, which in turn evolves into a new order?

This movement—orientation, disorientation, reorientation— is also discerned in the parables of Jesus. As but one example, in the parable of the prodigal son, the reader/listener is oriented to the story through the introduction of the central characters and the setting of the story. As the story unfolds, the reader/listener is jolted, shaken up, and disoriented in learning that the dutiful son appears to be treated unfairly by the father while the profligate son gets far more than his wayward behavior would merit. But the point of the parable is to reorient us to a radically new vision of unrestricted forgiveness and mercy that does not cancel out but perfects justice as it is ordinarily understood. The same may be said of the gospels taken as a whole.

In a similar vein, through the different instances of *kenosis* we have discussed, the kenotic pattern of Jesus' whole life and ministry can be discerned. As is to be expected, we begin at the beginning—in the Incarnation, with the vulnerable flesh of an infant laid low in a manger as the point of departure for tracing this kenotic pattern. But what if the kenotic pattern of the life and mission of Jesus were to be charted starting at the end of the continuing *kenosis*, beginning with the culmination and fulfillment of the self-emptying begun in the Incarnation?

The creedal affirmation that Christ descended to the dead between cross and resurrection is the optic through which we might better understand the kenotic pattern of Jesus' life mission. What is more, the descent is the interpretive key for understanding the fullness of the Paschal Mystery.

The *descensus* clause in the Apostles' Creed affirms that between cross and resurrection Christ dwelt among the dead. When and how did this affirmation emerge in the church of Christ? What possible meaning might it offer to those trying to live the Christian faith in our own day, quite often against all odds?

CHAPTER 4

From the Ash Heap

THE BELIEF THAT AT HIS DEATH on the cross and burial in the tomb Christ descended to the netherworld, to the bottoms, to the place of the dead, has been part of the church's faith from quite early on. However, in the main, this dimension of the faith has lain dormant in the ash heap, the dustbin of Christian theology, as well as in the life and prayer of the Christian people.

It is not at all uncommon for Christians today to recoil at the very notion of Christ descending to the dead, or into hell, as some interpretations have it. They are not alone. There have been efforts at different points in Christian history to erase the *descensus* clause, that Christ descended—among the dead or into hell—from the Apostles' Creed. Some devout Catholics admit that they button their lips at Mass when these words are prayed in the Apostles' Creed. Somewhat more palatable for many is the language of Christ's descent among the dead.

If asked about the meaning of the *descensus* clause, most Catholics today would be hard pressed to articulate even a remotely coherent understanding of these words. Indeed, the meaning of these few words is about as baffling as—perhaps more baffling than—the mystery of the Trinity to most. In fumbling attempts to explain the Trinity, God is often spoken of in numerical terms ending in vague and inchoate speech about the utter incomprehensibility of the divine mystery "up" in heaven for all eternity. But believers often don't know where or how to begin to explain Christ's descent. They will say that God is omnipotent and omnipresent and invisible, indeed everywhere. But in a voice both firm and overly confident they will assure you that God is most certainly not "down there." "Down there" is thought of as the region not of the dead but of the damned in hell, a "place" of eternal punishment—with eternity assumed to be a never-ending succession of twenty-four-hour days.

Should the belief in Christ's descent remain in the ash heap of theology? Why bother retrieving what seems to many to be better left on the dusty shelves of a theological library, something quite tangential to the faith of Christians? Indeed there are some who hold that the *descensus* clause is nothing more than a way of emphasizing, in the manner of a linguistic underline or verbal exclamation point, that Christ did truly die!

So why bother with it? There are at least two practical reasons for trying to retrieve the affirmation that Christ descended among the dead.

First, the church has a long tradition of attending to the reality of sin, the possibility of punishment for it, and our need for forgiveness and reconciliation. Images of hell course through Christian art, literature, poetry, and music and are deeply embedded in the Christian consciousness. In the sacramental life of the church, sin is understood to be cleansed in the waters of baptism. But, of course, sin does not end there. And so we must seek forgiveness for sin and reconciliation with God, with ourselves, with the church, and with all those against whom we have sinned. Then there are the practices of prayer, fasting, and almsgiving as one expresses sorrow for sin and a desire for true conversion of heart during Lent and perhaps at other specific times of the year. The celebration of the Eucharist—especially according to the revised Roman Missal of 2011—is replete, perhaps overburdened, with references to our sinfulness and our grievous faults.

Nothing, however, in the sacramental life of the church or in its wider liturgical practices explicitly expresses the truth of God's incalculable love for the dead. Yet this is precisely what belief in Christ's descent among the dead does. For this reason alone, belief in Christ's descent among the dead should not be allowed to remain shelved alongside other seemingly insignificant Christian beliefs. The fact that efforts throughout Christian history to remove it from the creed have failed is an indication that it is in no way tangential to the crux of Christian faith: cross and resurrection.

But there is a second equally—if not more—important reason. What if this vexing affirmation that Christ descended among the dead, rather than being a matter of interest to the odd theologian and marginal to Christian faith is, after all, a most comforting and pastoral Christian belief: that in his dying and death, in going to the bottoms of the netherworld, Christ embodies there God's unfathomable love for those who are facing death, for those who die, for the dead?

In the liturgical reforms following the Second Vatican Council, the regular use of the Nicene Creed in the celebration of the Mass had the unintended and unfortunate consequence of all but erasing the Apostles' Creed from the lips and hearts of the faithful. As it fell out of common liturgical use, many

Catholics grew unfamiliar with the Apostles' Creed. The Nicene Creed *normally* used on Sundays and solemnities became the *norm* for many. Those who continued the devotion of praying the Rosary remained familiar with the Apostles' Creed, with which the recitation of the Rosary begins, as did those Catholics well versed in the *Catechism of the Catholic Church*. But, in the main, the Apostles' Creed was no longer part of common Catholic vocabulary, certainly not in the language of the church's public worship.

In recent years, rank and file Catholics have increasingly expressed curiosity about Christ's descent. This is due in part to the "new" translation of the Roman Missal, which for so many priests and people is not a help but a hindrance to good liturgical celebration. But with the revised Roman Missal of 2011 the Apostles' Creed is prayed with greater frequency in the celebration of the Mass. There are those who prefer the Apostles' Creed because it is shorter than the Nicene Creed. A shorter creed can make for a quicker Mass! However, there is a nobler reason for professing the Apostles' Creed.

HISTORICAL INTERLUDE

Even though several centuries went by before it was finalized in written form, the Apostles' Creed captures a belief of the early church not found in the Nicene Creed: the *"descensus* clause," that at his death and interment Jesus Christ "descended to the dead" or, as it later came to be said, "descended into hell." This belief is not expressed in the Nicene Creed more familiar to most Catholics.

The Nicene-Constantinopolitan, or Nicene, Creed originated in the East, and was shaped by debates and discussion among those gathered at the first two ecumenical councils, held in the fourth century AD in Nicaea and Constantinople respectively. The Apostles' Creed in embryonic form (the Old Roman Creed) was already in use in Rome in the second century AD and has no single author. Nor is it the result of a collaborative writing project of the Twelve Apostles as its name might suggest to some. The Creed was committed to memory, not to writing. It does nonetheless provide testimony to what has been believed from the earliest days of the church in the West. In its definitive form, the Apostles' Creed emerged over the course of several hundred years, extending from the third through the eighth centuries. This process no doubt included efforts to define clearly and refine precisely. Through it all, the *descensus* clause was not eliminated, no small indicator of its vital place in Christian faith.

In the same way that each of the four gospels gives a particular reading of Jesus the Christ, with one or another gospel capturing more crisply what the other gospels do not, so too the two creeds prayed in the Roman Catholic Church from early on are complementary precisely because one expresses what the other does not, thereby providing a fuller expression of Christian faith. Alongside these creeds we might add the Athanasian Creed—widely accepted among the Christian churches in earlier centuries but used less and less frequently in public worship—which also includes the *descensus* clause.

AMONG THE DEAD OR INTO HELL?
Christians have long believed that at his death Christ descended to the netherworld, to the underworld—in Hebrew, Aramaic, and Syriac *Sheol* or in Greek *Hades*—to the bottoms, to the region of the dead. After his death on Calvary, Jesus was laid in the tomb, was a dead man, and descended to the dead,

to Sheol or Hades. Sheol is Sheol because God is absent from Sheol. Sheol is the "place," the "space," the "condition" of shadows where it is said that the living God is not. An awareness of Sheol or Hades as a region of lack of fulfillment, a condition of failure, a state of incompletion, has roots long, deep, and strong and is found in many different cultures. It connotes unpleasantness, and so is not desirable. But it is not understood as a state or place of eternal damnation where fiery flames burn and torture the soul irrevocably punished for sin. More akin to the later notion of purgatory, those in Sheol or Hades are not beyond hope. They endure. They wait.

By the second century, Christ's descent into Sheol or Hades was a well-attested belief referred to by Tertullian, Ignatius of Antioch, Polycarp, Justin, and Irenaeus. While many have looked to 1 Peter 3:19, "Christ went and made a proclamation to the spirits in prison" and Ephesians 4:9, which tells that Christ "descended to the lower regions" as providing scriptural grounds for the belief that he descended to the dead, it is quite possible that belief in Christ's descent emerged independently of these texts, and indeed may be earlier than 1 Peter. Perhaps the surest evidence for this primordial Christian belief is the very absence of the celebration of the Eucharist on Holy Saturday.

Are the "spirits in prison," those in the precincts of the dead, in hell? Answering this question calls for the introduction of Rufinus of Aquileia (c. 345–411)—monk, historian, theologian, and translator. It was through Rufinus that the words "descended into hell" found their way into the formulation of the Apostles' Creed. It was with Rufinus that the words of the *descensus* clause shifted from *ad inferos* (to the underworld as the region of the dead) to *ad inferna* (to hell as the region of the damned). With Rufinus we find the emergent tradition of the "harrowing of hell," that Christ did not simply rest among the dead but freed from hell the patriarchs and the just ones who lived before Jesus Christ.

Even though the descent *ad inferna* gained ascendency in the language of the church, it is important to recognize that the earlier form, *ad inferos*, does not convey the notion of punishment for sin and damnation as does the later form. "Hell" connotes damnation. "Hell" was prepared for Satan and his angels; it is Gehenna, the domain of the accursed. By contrast, Christ's descent to the dead bespeaks God's love in Christ reaching out to those waiting in anticipation of fulfillment, that is, the dead who endure, those who wait to hope.

The reasons for the shift from Christ's "descent to the dead" to his "descent into hell" would require a thorough historical examination well beyond what can be provided here. That the shift from "dead" to "hell" was never complete and that there remains a measure of interchangeability between these terms is demonstrated by the fact that "descent among the dead" remains in some renditions of the Apostles' Creed. Some Eastern liturgical texts use the language of descent into Hades. What is more, in the current Roman Rite, Eucharistic Prayer IV speaks of Christ's "descent to the realm of the dead."

The lines of the debate about the accuracy of the words "to the dead" and "into hell" can lead to a vexing point of confusion, as can an examination of the reasons why some in later centuries earnestly tried to remove the *descensus* clause from the Apostles' Creed. Here we simply note that it is curious that by the fourth century the phrase *descensus ad inferna* begins to appear in place of *descensus ad inferos* amidst a growing preoccupation with sin and the punishment for it, together with an increasingly pessimistic view of human nature commonly associated with Augustine's teaching on original sin. An overarching conviction about human sinfulness among some of the Fathers of the Church was fueled amidst fiery debates about the personhood of Christ, that is, one who is at once truly human and truly divine. Could God or would God really go to the regions of godlessness?

In the end it is best left to historians of the early church and to Patristics scholars to untangle the layers of discussion, debate, and disagreement that led to the change in language from *descendit ad inferos*—he descended to the dead—to *descendit ad inferna*—he descended to hell. Questions of *why* and *in what manner* Christ descended have been and remain the subject of debate and dispute, some quite vitriolic. Here we do not enter into the fray. The governing concern here is to demonstrate that an understanding of Christ's descent among the dead is the anchor of Christian hope replete with resources for living in the Spirit of God, the Spirit of Christ, especially in the times of darkness, dying, and death in which we live.

A question lingers: Would one willingly and knowingly change language that was expressive of the faith of the earliest Christians, especially the belief that God's restorative presence is found where God is thought not to be?

What, in the final account, are we saying when we affirm that Christ descended to the dead? At the very least, it is an affirmation that Jesus of Nazareth, Son and Word of the Father, did truly die and was buried, laid down in a tomb. He was a dead person (*nekros*) among the dead.

Is this, perhaps, the reason why the *descensus* clause has lain dormant in the theological ash heap? Is this why some would rather it remain there? Because if the affirmation that Christ descended among the dead is, as has sometimes been suggested, nothing more than a linguistic underline emphasizing the truth that Christ did truly die, that very emphasis draws attention to what most believers find unthinkable: the death of the incarnate God.

CHAPTER 5

The Death of the Incarnate God?

IN THE AFTERMATH of the Second World War, theologians such as Karl Barth, Jürgen Moltmann, and Eberhard Jüngel attended to the crucial significance of the death of Jesus for a Christian understanding of God. During this same period it was preeminently Hans Urs von Balthasar who devoted specific attention to the neglected creedal affirmation of Christ's descent into hell in its Trinitarian foundations as well as its implications for an adequate understanding of God. All of these theologians were aware of—and some were witness to—the devastating effects of war. In such a milieu there emerged a question that could not be ignored. That question is no less timely today: How is it possible not to take with utmost seriousness the world's godforsakeness and humanity's godlessness in trying to speak rightly of God? Mining what is embedded in the creedal affirmation that Christ did truly die, was interred, and descended among the dead is one way of taking that reality to heart.

If we are to take seriously the affirmation that Christ descended among the dead, that the incarnate God did truly die, at least two matters must be addressed. The first pertains to prevailing understandings of Christ; the second, to dominant views of the God beyond all knowing.

First, there is the matter of Christ's true humanity and true divinity. Far too often, thinking and speaking about Christ's descent have veered into the dangerous waters of focusing on one or the other "part" or "side" of Jesus, truly human and truly divine, descending among the dead. Even though it may seem a stretch for many, Christians are ready to believe that Christ's "human side" died and descended. But they are loath to think or say that his "divine side" died and descended among the dead or, worse, into hell.

Such seemingly rarified understandings are rooted in the Christological controversies of later centuries and not in the earliest strata of the apostolic witness of the church. But even taking the Christological formulations emerging from those controversies to heart, the notion of Jesus Christ consisting of parts or sides is wrongheaded and misses the mark. The aim of the Christological controversies was to affirm that Jesus of Nazareth, the Christ, Son and Word of the Father, is one person. He is not a "third thing" made up of two parts.

For the most part the two natures, human and divine, in the one person of Christ have been understood in a way that allows his human nature to be affected by the divine nature. While this is true, it must also be acknowledged Christ's divine nature is affected by his human nature. Thus we say of Jesus of Nazareth that he is the very life, light, and love of God, God's very self, speaking in a specifically human, fleshly way. His humanity and divinity interpenetrate one another. There is a cohesive bridge between the two natures so that Christ, truly human and divine in one person, is able to truly save humanity. But the offer of salvation in Christ is carried to its completion and then further in the descent, so that Christ continues to save humanity beyond the grave.

To suggest that on Calvary the "human side" of Jesus suffers, dies, and is buried, but that his "divine side" is spared all of this necessarily leads to the conclusion that the mystery of the Incarnation is suspended, or held in abeyance. If there be even a hint of truth in this claim, then flesh-and-blood mortal human beings are not saved in and by Christ.

If we are honest with ourselves, the prevailing image we have inherited from the tradition is that Jesus of Nazareth, the Crucified One, "dies and flies." As he breathes his last, he simultaneously goes to heaven. We have a hard time believing that Jesus really experienced the fullness of death, our death. We can recognize that he knew the depths of human despair, the pain of the cross, the loneliness of friends leaving his side, the sorrow of seeing the tears of his mother. This is to say nothing of the physical pain inflicted on him. Yet, when he dies upon the cross, it is tempting for us to imagine him waking up in heaven from a momentary slumber, the mortal life a bad dream, the phase of his humanity over and done. This perception of Jesus as one who dies and flies immediately to heaven blinds us to the reality that this one person, Jesus the Christ, did truly die. Such a view inadvertently undercuts the truth that the Christ was a corpse, was mourned by his followers, and was laid in a tomb. There is silence, grief, desolation, disappointment. The pain of this experience of the followers of Jesus cannot be glossed over, as is all too often done because of what is now believed is yet to come on the third day. Did the disciples know what was yet to come? If yes, then why such astonishment, indeed disbelief, on the third day? Did Jesus himself have certain knowledge of what awaited him after his death? His final words from the cross were those of a son abandoned and forsaken by his father: "Why have you abandoned me?" Yet still trusting in the Father: "Into your hands I commend my spirit"—both echoes of Psalm 22.

The suffering of Jesus the Christ was not unlike the worst kind of human suffering. It was in no way lessened because what some think of as the divine "part" did not, indeed could not, suffer and die. Or because of some supposed foreknowledge that he knew exactly how the Father's promise would unfold, with him in a sparkling white robe, the heavy stone rolled away, the amazed disciple Mary of Magdala who ran ahead to tell Peter and the other disciple about the empty tomb—she who was one of the few who remained faithful to the end, and then after. Jesus dies. Death is inevitable for all who dwell on the earth. There is no escaping it. And death is not a partial experience, even for the incarnate God.

The common misunderstanding that Jesus on the cross "dies and flies" is bolstered by the gospel narrative of the exchange between the Christ dying on the cross and the one called the Good Thief, or Dismas in some Christian traditions. In contrast to the hardened and cynical thief crucified on the other side of Jesus, the Good Thief, who no doubt has run out of chances, risks one final gamble in the hope of one last chance. He recognizes that he has squandered his life and is now getting his just deserts. He sees no wrong in Jesus, and he asks that Jesus remember him when he comes into his kingdom. Jesus assures him: This day you will be with me in paradise.

A quick reading or hearing of the words of Jesus lends to the understanding that he promises the Good Thief that he will be with him today, that is, within the next twenty-four hours. But on further reflection "this day" is most likely not a reference to a twenty-four-hour period. Rather, Jesus is speaking of that day when the kingdom is fully ushered in. It is on this day that the Good Thief will be with Jesus in paradise. It is this day of the kingdom, when the promises of God are fulfilled, when the blind shall see, the lame shall leap, the poor shall eat and have their fill. It is a moment, not measured by instants, seconds, minutes, hours, or years, when every tear shall be wiped away, when the time will come for singing and death will be no more.

That Jesus does not die and fly in an instant was well known by the earliest followers. Their belief was passed from generation to generation in sermons of the early Church Fathers who wrote of Christ in the tomb, in iconography that depicts Christ descending to the dead and being raised to glory in one scene, a single movement at once into the depths and into glory. Most important, the reality of Christ's death and descent is commemorated on Holy Saturday. On this day there are no shouts of joy and gladness. There is silence. As is fitting. It is a day of darkness. The heart is heavy with sadness. For Christ, this day is among the dead, bringing the good news to the dead that death is no more for those who wait in hope.

A second challenge raised by the death of Christ pertains to prevailing understandings of God. Does the death of the incarnate God affect the very life of God?

Here it is of the utmost importance to remember that theology and doctrine serve a story. This story is none other than the gospel. And at the heart of the gospel is the narrative of the three days: Friday, Saturday, and Sunday. These tell of the crucifixion, dying/death/interment, and raising to new life of the Crucified One.

As this message was heard and passed on to later generations, questions emerged about the nature of the relationship of Father and Son and Spirit, propelled by a fundamental question about God: If Jesus is the Son of God, indeed himself divine, did God then truly suffer and die?

Early efforts to answer this question relied on philosophical tools at hand. Foremost among them was a worldview that held in opposition the temporal and the eternal, the visible and the invisible, matter and spirit and, above all, the perishable and the imperishable. The church has labored under the burden of this dualism from the time of its expansion beyond the small reach of Jesus' ministry: God's being is the antithesis of ours. God is all that humans are not; eternity is the opposite of the temporal; immortality is incompatible with perishability. God does not change, but we do. God is stable; we are contingent. God is spirit; mortals are flesh.

If theology and doctrine are to serve the story of the God who becomes incarnate and is interred, then this view of God must be reconsidered. Divine immutability (that God cannot change) and divine impassibility (that God is not affected by anything other than or outside God) are notions difficult to sustain in light of the affirmation that God does in fact do this in Jesus Christ.

Here theology and doctrine that are bound, indeed chained, by an inert metaphysical dualism must bow and conform to the story of the crucifixion, death, burial, descent, and raising up of the Crucified One. The most crucial ingredient of Christian faith is its most shocking: in Jesus, son of Mary and son of the Father and the church's Risen One, God was not only incarnate but interred.

The God whose very life is given to us in becoming one of us even in death, is given to us completely and irrevocably, but does not cease to be God. What appears to be impossible for God—embracing perishability and death—is proclaimed by the gospel to be possible. It is in remaining God while being subjected to perishability that God's true immutability consists. In the incarnation and interment, God's freedom to embrace humanity in its entirety is not diminished or negated. Rather God's embrace of death is fulfillment, plentitude, and superabundance of the divine nature. It is not the divine nature that is contradicted between cross and resurrection, but all human ideas about what God can, cannot, and—indeed—may not do.

This entails yielding to the gospel truth that from God's own suffering and death in the Son and Word, a new and creative act of the Father in the Spirit springs forth: the crucified Christ is raised from death and nothingness.

In God's unfathomable generosity, love not only reaches and embraces our dying and death, but descends to the nadir of our wretchedness and tragedy.

Divine love suffers, but not in a way that limits God's freedom. Rather, this love exemplifies freedom by willingly entering into the suffering of humanity and of all creation. It may be properly understood as a willing, active suffering that in no way limits the otherness or beyondness of God. To doubt the authenticity of Christ's suffering and death on the cross (or, in more theoretical terms, to yield to the slightest hint of the heresy of Docetism) leads to the denial of the salvific work begun in the Incarnation.

There is a font of Christian wisdom embedded in the maxim of Gregory Nazianzus: "What is not assumed is not redeemed." It bespeaks the truth that what Jesus the Christ does not take on, or into, himself is not healed, is not transformed, is not set right. If Jesus the Christ is not truly human, then we are not truly saved. Jesus takes on our humanity, not just maleness, and so all human beings, male and female, are to be made new through him. By his becoming one of us, a mortal, everyone and everything that lives is quickened by God's creative and sanctifying love enfleshed in Christ. So too with our dying and death. Christ brings the good news that death is no more, that the power of love will prevail over all evil. And he goes so far and yet farther still, deep down into the depths, to bring this news to the precincts of the dead. Yes, the news is brought even to those who may seem to be without hope, indeed beyond hope.

In an earlier chapter attention was drawn to the necessity of recognizing that our efforts to speak of life beyond death lie in a remote region of approximation rather than literalistic certitude. In a similar way, anything meaningful or truthful that is said of God is said with no small measure of reticence as an approximation.

In speaking of the suffering, death, and descent of the incarnate God, our words give way to wonder in the recognition that the suffering and death of the incarnate God is unlike any other suffering and death. It is not human suffering and death to the nth degree. It can be spoken of only in negative terms: the death of the incarnate God is unlike any human death. The unfathomable self-emptying of God unto death, a death that goes even deeper than the deepest precincts of the dead, and yet deeper still, is of an altogether different kind.

Perhaps the best way of coming to an adequate, rather than exhaustive, understanding of the altogether different death of the incarnate God is through the lens of the dynamic interaction of God's transcendence and immanence. Often thought to be opposites, in God's transcendence (beyond) God is infinitely present (here). There are echoes of this in Augustine's *Confessions* Book X where he speaks of God as nearer to me than I am to myself.

It is through utter transcendence that God is altogether present to suffering. Precisely as transcendent, God is more present to human suffering than I am in my own suffering. Because this is God suffering as God, it is a suffering of a different order from any human suffering. Thus God does not suffer in the way we think of suffering, because it is God suffering as God. God knows suffering more deeply and fully than we do because God knows suffering as God.

But there is more. And here we find that, with all of its limitations, the language of two natures in the one person of Jesus Christ should not be jettisoned altogether. There is deep insight here in the face of what the mind cannot truly grasp: there are two modes of consciousness in Jesus Christ. God chooses to participate in human suffering in a particular humanity. God willingly and freely suffers with a human consciousness—that of Jesus the Christ who does truly suffer and die. So God knows suffering as God knows, and in Jesus Christ God knows suffering as we know it.

Do we speak rightly of God in speaking of the death of the incarnate God? If Jesus' body is God's body, then Jesus' death is God's death.

CHAPTER 6

Bringing Comfort

IS THE RETRIEVAL OF THE MEANING of Christ's descent and the theological challenges it presents to prevailing understandings of God purely a matter of speculative interest? Is it just one more theological exercise that has no "takeaway" for those who are simply trying to come to a deeper understanding of their faith and put it into practice in their day-to-day lives?

In an age driven by a near-obsession with results, with the bottom line, with assessing and measuring outcomes, there is widespread distrust of theological reflection. Theology is judged to be a lofty and speculative exercise, a pie-in-the-sky enterprise that makes no difference in the everyday life of the Christian. Many are skittish, if not outright distrustful, of probing theological questions, especially one as vexing as the mystery of Christ's descent.

But it is useful to recall that throughout the centuries those theologians who made a mark on Christian history and spirituality did their work with the practical needs of Christians, of the living church, in the forefront of their minds. In considering ancient church writers and teachers such as John Damascene, Gregory of Nyssa, Tertullian, or Athanasius, it must be recognized that their theological writing was done with pastoral intent in the face of new questions, in light of shifting modes of perceiving and being.

Athanasius' preeminent concern with the Incarnation—the truth that God had spoken and is speaking in human flesh—gave rise to a sustained argument against any effort to denigrate human flesh, a prevalent tendency during his time.

Thomas Aquinas' *Summa Theologica* is a systematic treatment of God's relationship to the world and everything in it in terms of *exitus et reditus*—everything and everyone being from God and returning back to God, with divine providence ordering all things, and with the wisdom of God in Christ as the key. But the medieval Aquinas was not writing in a vacuum. He was teaching students in the new Order of Preachers as they were being prepared for the practical work of preaching and hearing confessions.

This practical intent is also found in the work of Thomas Aquinas' contemporary, Bonaventure, whose focus was on Christ among us in *il poverello*, Christ Crucified in the flesh of Francis of Assisi.

In the twentieth century, Karl Rahner's effort to recover the humanity of Christ was in no small measure motivated by his awareness of the devastating forces of dehumanization fueled by political forces in his native Germany. He clearly saw the need for dialogue among persons based on a common hope for better humanity, prescinding from but without dismissing the matter of the particular religious beliefs held by them.

Jürgen Moltmann's theology of hope and the crucified God likewise emerged as a result of the Second World War. But, unlike Rahner, who spent the war years teaching and doing pastoral work in Vienna, Moltmann was incarcerated during the war and was eyewitness to its horrors. As a result of his prison experience, during which he was tormented, bereft of all hope, and experienced being forsaken by God, he was led to quite different conclusions about the suffering of God than was Rahner. Moltmann came to believe and think about a God who is not unmoved by suffering, who knows suffering, and who is a God of consolation, not apathy.

Also a prisoner during World War II, Yves Congar in its aftermath focused on John 17 in an ecumenical context, forging a path of unity for Christians separated from one another by years of discord.

In our own day, Catherine Mowry La Cugna has left a legacy of retrieving and revitalizing the relationality at the very heart of the divine life—a relationality that affects our relationship not only with God but also with the other, others, every living creature, the whole of creation and the cosmos.

The contemporary Catholic feminist theologian, Elizabeth Johnson, has taken stock of the concrete experience of women in the quest for more adequate understandings that invite us to speak rightly of God in more expansive ways, always within the context of the Catholic tradition that allows for images of God as both female and male.

What all of these efforts go to show is that while theology is primarily about God, it is also about us. Every Christian belief expresses in some way a truth about what it takes to make good on the one and only life we have to live.

Consider Mary. In speaking and teaching about Mary, the church is indeed speaking in the first place about Miriam of Nazareth, Mary the mother of Jesus. But in formulating the dogmas of the Immaculate Conception and the Assumption, the church is also articulating an understanding of itself. In saying that Mary was preserved from sin from the beginning of her life until the end, and that she was taken in her entirety into heaven, the church is expressing its belief that from its origins to its end, she, the church, is under God's protection and will endure until the power of love prevails over all evil.

While belief in Christ's descent has largely drawn and continues to draw half-hearted if not outright negative responses, it is possible that a proper understanding of it might gain a warmer reception. This creedal affirmation is, after all, a rich pastoral resource that may bring comfort to those facing into death, as well as to those who accompany the dying as they make passage through death to what lies beyond the grave. Understanding the practical import of the descent entails recognizing that, while the descent is primarily a truth about Christ, it is also about us mortals of any and every epoch who pass, pass away, make passage, die.

Is Christ's descent an event entirely in the past? It is, in the same way that the life, ministry, passion, and death of Jesus are past events in history. But it is not when it is viewed in light of the effects of the Paschal Mystery. Is not the Pasch of Christ rendered present in word and sacrament as we live toward death in the hope that the power of love shall prevail over all evil? Is not the reason for our hope anchored in the conviction that Christ did truly die, was interred, and that the Crucified One who died and was buried now lives and breathes anew—in us? God is not restricted by past, present, or future.

As we have seen, when Christ's descent is understood in terms of "into hell" more than "among the dead," the focus is on the just who had come before him and had not received the grace offered through him. Some depictions of the resurrection, however, portray Jesus coming up from the darkness of the netherworld, taking Adam and Eve by the hand with him up to the heavens. But Adam and Eve do not signify only the righteous ones who lived virtuous lives in the past as they waited for the coming of the Savior. Adam and Eve here signify the whole of the human race, the entirety of humanity.

A revitalized understanding of the descent among the dead allows us to see God's loving reach to the netherworld, to the place of the dead, as not being confined to the past. It is effective here and now. In descending to the dead, God in Christ refuses to take the human "no" for an answer. God reaches down, as it were, and takes the dead to himself. Through the descent to the dead, God's love in Christ reunites past, present, and future. God's love brings the living and the dead into the communion of the Three in One Love, together with those who are yet to live and those who are yet to die.

It is easy to understand why we think of Christ's death, descent, and resurrection as three separate events: one takes place on Friday, the next on Saturday, and then finally the last on Sunday morning. Indeed the gospel accounts of the Lord's Pasch reach from Thursday evening through Sunday morning. And so we think of Christ in the tomb, his descent, as somewhere between the cross and the resurrection. But these three are inseparable: death, descent, and resurrection. The iconography of the Christian East expresses this visually. The Eastern Christian icons of the resurrection do not depict Jesus rising from an antiseptically empty tomb. There are no spring flowers, no angels, and no Easter sunshine peeks up over Calvary. Rather, these icons depict the glorified Jesus clothed in brightest white, in the very heart of Hades, surrounded by his and our ancestors in faith. Critically important in these depictions is the reality that the descent is not only the lowest point of kenotic humiliation but is also the first point of elevation. Christ's being among the dead is light in their darkness.

In Christ, God's merciful reach extends not only to those who had not or have not heard the gospel, but also to those who for whatever reason were, or are, indisposed or unable to hear the good news addressed to them. God reaches down, as it were, and takes the dead to himself. No language other than that of the descent among the dead, the *descensus* clause, is capable of expressing the incalculable depth of the reach by which the whole world and everything in it is embraced and held close to the very heart of the God whose name above all naming is Mercy. God's very life is the love that pours itself forth to the bottoms, to the netherworld, in mercy.

The practical import of a revitalized understanding of Christ's descent bears on three different deaths, or three different experiences of death: (1) physical death, (2) spiritual death, and (3) regions of death within myself.

PHYSICAL DEATH

Faith in the descent reveals that God is one with us in dying and in death. Indeed, God cares for the dead. Into the very domain of death, life enters and conquers the forces of death. The descent affirms that a human being is not left alone in this world to cope with conflict and turmoil. When with the Psalmist (130:1) we cry out of the depths, we are asking that God descend, that God draw near us in our brokenness and weakness, that God come to our assistance with a healing balm for our wounds.

No matter how severe the suffering I may endure, Christ himself has known such torment. Jesus Christ has shared our experience of death and has been delivered from its jaws. Christ has so shared our hell that we do not have to endure it alone. What may bring comfort is the knowledge that God's love and care do not end with death, that even there God is present. In proclaiming Christ's descent to the dead, the tradition testifies to God as being one with humanity even in death.

No matter how excruciating my suffering, no matter how unspeakable the pain of a person or a people, Christ has also known such horror. For Karl Barth, because of the descent, any desperation we may experience is not the total desolation suffered by Jesus Christ alone in being forsaken, abandoned on the cross by the Father.

Further, we are able to bring some small comfort to those facing into death with the assurance that whatever awaits them at the end of their mortal life, the love of God in Christ which knows no bounds is there. Even there. The awareness that through Christ's descent our hell is defeated may give assurance and bring consolation to anyone facing into death. As we make passage at the time we draw our last breath, we enter a geography through which Christ himself has passed.

Preaching to those in mourning on the occasion of his brother's funeral in the fourth century, Ambrose focused on Christ's descent. Martin Luther counseled those who fear death to "gaze at . . . Christ, who descended into hell," for hell is defeated by Christ's sharing our experience of death.

After asking why the words "he descended into hell" are in the Creed, the *Heidelberg Catechism* provides this answer:

That in my severest tribulations I may be assured that Christ my Lord has redeemed me from hellish anxieties and torments by the unspeakable anguish, pains and terrors which he suffered in his soul both on the cross and before. (Response to Question 44)

Affirming that Christ descended to the dead expresses the belief that there is no division between the living and the dead but, rather, there exists the deepest kind of communion between them. No small comfort. There is an inseparable bond between us and those who have gone before us—and those who are yet to come. The creedal affirmation of the communion of saints expresses our belief that particular men and women who have walked the face of the earth among other mortals—men and women such as Catherine of Siena, Lorenzo Ruiz, Thérèse of Lisieux, John of the Cross, Katharine Drexel—are now among the blessed who populate the many mansions of the home we call heaven. We speak to them. We ask them to help us, because they are near to God and can come to our aid in times of need. They can bring us comfort and solace, healing and consolation in trying times. We designate some as patrons of our specific concerns: Anthony of Padua is invoked to help us find items we have misplaced or lost; Jude for what are judged to be impossible cases—and those people we find utterly impossible! Katharine Drexel is invoked for improved relations between and among various races; Francis of Assisi, in our efforts to take better care of Mother Earth, our common home. These are a few of those many hundreds who have been named "Saint" by the church. Then there are those who are named Blessed, or Venerable, or Servant of God.

But what of those virtuous, indeed saintly, people we have known whose names will likely never be inscribed in the church's book of saints? And what is to be said of those who did not lead virtuous lives; those whose lives were unfinished, unfulfilled; those who lacked the knowledge or the strength or the mental health to make good on the life they were given? And what about those who were so desperate that their last best hope for something better than their own suffering and pain was to seek relief by taking their own life? Christ's descent to and among the dead serves as a reminder to all the living that we are bonded to them as well as to the blessed in heaven. They are never very far from us in the deepest kind of communion.

Another practical implication of the mystery of Christ's descent that is worthy of attention is one that may be particularly pertinent to people in our part of today's world. It is now a commonplace to hear that we in the West have been shaped by a culture which, while insisting that nothing is more important than family, prizes individualism over all else. Unlike other cultures that still have a strong network of nuclear and extended family, we tend to think of ourselves first as individuals with rights and liberties to be exercised freely and without constraint. But there is at least one fault line in the exercise of unbridled freedom. Many of us are growing old alone. Even those who have had the advantage of good family relationships end up alone as their children and their grandchildren juggle many competing duties and responsibilities, sometimes at a great distance. It is easy enough to see that many seniors, our elders, fear becoming forgetful through cognitive impairment and dementia in its many forms. But perhaps the deeper fear, unnamed yet coursing through the veins of everyone who grows old alone—and even some who are graced with the presence of friends and family—is the fear of being forgotten by others: My life does not matter. I will be forgotten.

A consequence of the belief in Christ's descent among the dead is that we may rest assured that, though others do forget us after death, in God's unfathomable generosity, the dead are never forgotten. We keep memory of military heroes of World War I, of World War II, of the Vietnam War, of saints, of grandparents, and of our beloved dead. But the mind stretches back only so far, and can grasp only so much in the waves of millions upon millions of mortals who have dwelt on the earth. Facing into our own death, or accompanying a beloved friend, spouse, or family member as they near the end of the only life they have ever known, it is no small comfort to know that not one living soul who has been, or shall ever be, is or will be forgotten by God.

To our minds the dead are not here. They are gone. But because of the depth of God's reach they are not gone and are never forgotten. The descent of Christ to the dead bespeaks the truth that God remembers even those who live in the darkness of death. Their lives were and are by God's hand. Nothing, and no one, is beyond God's reach.

Jesus did truly die, as is true for all and everything of the earth. So no one who lives and dies in communion with Jesus, trusting and hoping in him, need die alienated from God anymore. In communion with Jesus, our dying loses its desolation and is turned into a death in hope. This fundamental Christian truth is expressed unambiguously in words of Paul: "In life and in death we are the Lord's" (Romans 14:8).

Christ's descent means that God is with us in a manner that is beyond what we might ever have imagined. Jesus the Christ does not simply slide through the region of the dead in the way that a driver with an Easy Pass account breezes through the tollbooth on the highway or at the bridge. By

Christ's descent among the dead, God's love in Christ enters into solidarity with the dead, for he has truly died. Love itself transforms death into Sabbath rest in God's presence. Thus we may say of our beloved dead, as well as of those who are far beyond our ability to love and those we may have judged to have died outside the embrace of God: May they rest in peace.

No Christian escapes death. Christ's descent assures us that God's life continues in death, that God's goodness and generosity continue after the individual's mortal life is finished. The descent addresses the inevitability of death, linking it with the consolation of God's presence as we face into death and accompany others to death's door. More, the belief that God's love in Christ has penetrated the dark abyss between the living and the dead can bring consolation to those who mourn. There is no "place," "space," or "condition" where God in Christ has not gone and will not go with the offer of light, love, and life. Absolutely nothing is beyond the reach of God's mercy. The love of God penetrates even and especially the hearts of those who sit in darkness. Any desolation or darkness we may know has been suffered and transformed by Jesus Christ.

In proclaiming Christ's descent to the dead, the tradition testifies to God as one with humanity even in death. Faith in the descent reveals that God is one with the dead, cares for the dead. In the face of death the Christian may know that God's love and care do not end at our dying and death—that, even there, God is.

SPIRITUAL DEATH

In considering the practical import of belief in the descent, it is crucial to understand that the dead to whom Christ brings

God's love are not only the physically dead, but also those in the land of the living who are without hope, those in darkness and unable to find the light.

It is common to hear and to see the anguish of parents whose children seem to have lost their way in life. Consider the father who has never really managed to get past the guilt he feels as a result of his good girl gone bad. Seeing the catastrophe unfolding in the life of his mentally ill, alcoholic sister, a brother is powerless in the face of the destruction she has wrought in the family, in the lives of loved ones, and in the lives of others beyond numbering. She is dead, even as her mortal body dwells on the earth. Is it possible that belief in Christ's descent among the dead might offer some stirring of new life here? Might belief in Christ's descent into hell speak to the spiritually dead? For Christ's death was not make-believe; he was truly dead. But the one called Father brought life from that tomb.

Consider the unspeakable anguish of the parents whose son has taken his own life. They worry endlessly that his soul may be in hell. But, wherever their son may be in the ocean of God's mercy, it is they who are living in hell here and now on earth, tormented every day, indeed tormenting themselves, with guilt and remorse. They are among the walking dead. Their grief can hardly find words. Can the mystery of Christ's descent among the dead bring a word of comfort to them? For Christ too descended into the region of the dead. He was a dead man, *nekros*, among the dead. And life came from death. From among the dead.

Such situations are manifestations of spiritual death. We agonize when we see those we love lifeless, desperately in need of a balm that might soothe and rejuvenate their spirits.

Our encounters with the myriad deaths of spirit wrought by addictions of all sorts, by greed, narcissism, violence, and the abuse of power cause us to recoil. We are at once saddened and shocked by the realization that spiritual death is death nonetheless.

But we are sometimes much too quick to point to the manifestations of spiritual death in others without taking stock of a deeply unsettling truth: it is often the case that we ourselves are walking around spiritually dead, simply going through the motions of living a Christian life while we exist, but are not really alive.

DEAD SPACES WITHIN

Often we ourselves are among the living dead because of very deep wounds lodged in us from early childhood, blocked from our own view and hidden from others. They begin to manifest themselves in all-consuming anxiety, uncontrollable rage, and anger. These are often directed at those we love and those who love us. And then there is the guilt we carry through the years for what we have done and not done. Who has not known the hurt of being called by some demeaning name as a child, a hurt that causes a festering sore in the soul? Such hurts are buried deep in each and every one of us. Perhaps there are exceptions. But these are rare. The cumulative effect of such wounding and hurt can result in the dying and death of one's own spirit.

That we may not be aware of these deep-down wounds within, or flatly deny or ignore them, is precisely the problem. Taking Gregory Nazianzus' insight that what is not assumed is not redeemed to the very practical level: what is not named is not healed. Or, in the light of the gospel, that which is hidden, or concealed, is to be revealed so as to be redeemed.

In what may seem a stretch here, one of the recurrent themes of Pope Francis' ministry relates to these dead spaces, these long forgotten wounds in our own hearts and in the hearts of others. Prior to his election to the Chair of Peter, Cardinal Jorge Mario Bergoglio, Archbishop of Buenos Aires, introduced the notion of "existential peripheries." When addressing the cardinal electors on the eve of the conclave from which he would emerge as the Bishop of Rome, he spoke of the need for the church to look outward, to cease being self-referential in order that it might be fueled by zeal for the church's mission. He stated plainly that if the church continues to look ceaselessly inward, it will sicken. The church, rather, is to reach out with the good news to the existential peripheries.

On first hearing these words, it seems that Francis has in mind those who are at the edges, the margins, the fringes, the periphery of society and church because of poverty or of ethnic, racial, linguistic, or cultural inequity. To this might be added people with mental or physical disability, for whom he has shown a predilection, as well as the frail elderly, or those who are cast to the margins because of sexual orientation or because of religious persuasion. While all of these may be understood as persons and groups at the periphery, in his address to the cardinal electors, his emphasis was on no one particular group of people. The peripheries here do not refer to the location of those cast aside because of poverty. These are *existential* peripheries: sin, misery, ignorance, indifference, injustice.

Francis' concern may well be preeminently with those who are materially poor and with the plethora of impoverishments that such poverty causes. But sin, misery and pain, indifference, and ignorance are no strangers to any of us.

The descent of Christ bespeaks the love of God going to the peripheries of our own awareness, to the dregs of our own consciousness. God's love reaches down and out to the farthest places, the spaces we have forgotten and then forget that we have forgotten: our own anguish, the suffering inflicted on us by others and the sufferings we have caused in ourselves through our inordinate attachment to any of the magnificent distractions and diversions we need so badly to keep from facing our own spiritual disease.

Francis likens the church to the moon. The church is to reflect not itself but Christ, in the way that the moon reflects the light of the sun, so that the light of Christ may reach out and into the mystery of sin, of pain, of injustice, of ignorance. We too readily think of those at the margins as people and groups out there, over there, the ones who are so easily forgotten. They are not on our "radar screen." Thus Francis's message is thought to pertain only to them. But the church's mission is to allow Christ's light to penetrate the peripheries, those places or spaces that are not far from us and are often to be searched out in our own hidden, hurting, dead hearts.

Recall that even though he bears the name of Francis of Assisi, Bergoglio was schooled in the spirit of Ignatius Loyola, always alert to the movements of the Spirit and spirits in the deepest recesses of his own heart and the hearts of others. Bergoglio's own experience of God's mercy reaching into the bottoms, down to the unconverted corners, or edges, of his own heart is enshrined in his episcopal and now papal motto: *Miserando atque eligendo*. Taken from the twenty-first homily of Bede the Venerable on the calling of Matthew, the motto is best translated as "By mercifully choosing" or, perhaps, "By God's merciful choice." There is little doubt that these words were chosen by Bergoglio in remembrance of God's mercy toward him in choosing him in his lowliness, amidst the concrete circumstances of his own sinful life.

What of the peripheries of our own existence, the dead spaces in our own lives where the light of Christ has yet to enlighten, enliven, and guide us? Who among us has not known pain, ignorance, indifference? Who has not seen the ugly face of sin deep within?

When our wounds are not known and named, they cannot be soothed and healed. Our sickness and sin are passed on to others so that the web of brokenness and woundedness expands to gather more and more in its paralyzing grip.

Digging around the dregs, in the dead spaces, of my own life is very lonesome work. Looking for signs of life amidst the rubble of my own doing can be haunting and horrifying. But it can be healing if and when I recognize that I do not do this all alone. Belief in the descent means that Christ brings good news to the most unlikely of places, ugly spaces, those deathly spots in the hidden recesses of the heart. Because Christ brings comfort and consolation even there, facing the deepmost depth of ourselves, we find the strength born of the certain knowledge that the human heart is a region not only of wound, but also of wisdom.

At the edge of comprehension we glimpse God's love in the deepest center of ourselves and open up and out to the circles of suffering and hell on earth from which the many millions of mortals today cry out for release. We boldly believe that the love of God reaches even there. Amidst the embers of our shattered lives and loves, there is the warm balm of the Crucified One. Christ's soothing unction strengthens our dry and aching bones—yes even our brittle, old, broken bones—

bringing comfort in the knowledge that in our darkest hour, when we are falling into the pit whose bottom has no bottom, God will reach even farther to find us.

God enters our life at its most vulnerable point—where the vestiges of light, love, and life are being threatened with extinction, and in some cases may have already been snuffed out. Belief in the descent affirms that God's reach is so deep that even the regions of death in our own lives are seized and saturated by God's love in Christ through the gift of the Spirit. Indeed it is true that where there is life there is hope. But the descent among the dead affirms that there is hope even in death.

The belief in Christ's descent has very practical implications. When we face into our own death, the death of those we love, or our beloved dead; when we grieve the spiritual death of the living dead in our midst; when we find the courage to recognize the dead spaces in our own lives we can act, bolstered by the certain knowledge that the presence and power of the Spirit of God, the Spirit of Christ are at work even and especially there. And thus there is hope for the dead.

CHAPTER 7

Hope for the Dead?

APART FROM THE CROSS the resurrection has no meaning. At the heart of the cruciform mystery of Christian living, new life is found. Or given.

It is far too common to allow our thoughts to leapfrog from the Friday to the Sunday, without giving due attention to the second day of Christ's passage, the seventh day of the week, the Saturday. Yet, strange as it may seem, in the language and logic of gift, it is precisely in this place of emptiness, loss, grief, and darkness, in the forgotten liminal space between the first and the third day, in the gaping nothingness between the last day—on the cross—and the first day of new life—in the glory of the resurrection—that we find the firmest anchor for an understanding of Christian hope. Here our attention turns to the multiple meanings of hope.

"Hope" is a slippery word with multiple meanings. The English language fails to capture the richly layered meanings in this word. In some other languages, however, different words express different layers of the meaning of hope. In French, *espoir* expresses a hope that is more like a wish. The term would be used to express the hope that it doesn't rain on our picnic or snow when we travel at Christmastime. We might hope to do well in a job interview. We can also hope our health holds when we have responsibilities to fulfill, or hope that our loved ones are protected from illness or an accident, or that a friend's surgery is successful. Here we draw closer to the deeper meanings of hope expressed in the French *esperance*—hope as a movement within us that sees the present and all its prospects, or lack thereof, in the light of another possibility, something good, or even slightly better, that is to come. It recognizes that what is presently possible might not be all that there is. Hope looks in anticipation toward some other—a person, a thing, an event, a time, or a state—in the realization that if and when it does come, it can only come as a gift.

Hope is at the very heart, the core of a human being. There is nothing more central to human life. It is the driving force of all human initiative, the undercurrent of all human activity. It impels and propels. It looks for the coming of the new, that which has never been before. Hope is the dynamism that carries us from now to then, inclining us to look from the present to the future, from what is to what is still to come, and on to what might yet be. Hope is dynamism of the human person *in via*, on the way. Hope is squandered in despair as resignation to failure, and in presumption as cocksure certitude of fulfillment. Both are betrayals of hope, by which we try to deny our existence as voyagers, wanting instead to control and so to guarantee what lies ahead.

The deepest kind of hope is rooted in the conviction that there is still more to be said and that there might yet be some good news. Hope waits and yearns. It is not restlessness. It is more akin to anticipation than expectation.

Hope at this deeper level of *esperance* is not optimism. It should not be equated with the lightheartedness we might feel when things appear to be going our way. It is not what motivates us to put our time and energy into someone or something that has a good chance of succeeding. Rather, hope is the serene conviction that something is worth whatever I have to give, regardless of how it might turn out.

The more desperate the situation in which we demonstrate hope, the more forbidding the circumstances, the greater the odds against things turning out well, the deeper the hope. The more hopeless the present may appear to be, the more ardent our hope for something better.

Hope is not static. Hope strains ahead, impelled by the conviction that there may be a way out of whatever difficulty is at hand, that things can work out even though it may seem unlikely. Hope is that inextricable sense of the possible, of what might be. Hope is always directed toward a future good that is hard but not absolutely impossible to attain. Hope longs to find or to make a path past every dead end. Hope grows stronger as our last resource seems to fail us, when we come undone in the face of a situation that seems without possibility. Even if we are stopped dead in our tracks, hope seeks a way forward.

CHRISTIAN HOPE

In a specifically Christian sense, hope is one of three theological virtues. Sandwiched between faith and love, hope is like the proverbial middle child who does not get the same measure of attention as the others. It is common for Christians to appeal to the writings of Paul in asserting that while in the end three things last—faith, hope and love—the "greatest of these is love" (1 Corinthians 13:13). But hope does last; it does endure. And it is of a piece with faith and love. Indeed there is a great deal of overlap among the three. On the one hand there is considerable similarity between hope, confidence, and trust, although confidence and trust are often associated with faith. On the other hand, hope is akin to desire, wanting, and long-ing, which are most often associated with love.

The distinctions we make among the three theological virtues only serve to help us understand different dimensions of a single reality, one gift that makes possible our deepening relationship with God as well as our response to this gift.

So, is there anything distinctive about hope? Is there some-thing about the human person and the relationship between the human person and God that is properly named "hope," in contrast to what we name "faith" and "love"?

In general, theologians in the Christian tradition have maintained that hope rests on what has already been affirmed by faith. Faith makes the first move. The Christian says, "Yes, I accept, I do believe," and hope is put in what has been affirmed. We live out what is believed and hoped through charity, or love.

In other terms, faith is a movement of the intellect. Chari-ty is action. Hope is the energy that impels, propels them both.

Taking to heart the insights of Karl Rahner, we can say that hope undergirds both faith and love. Hope is the very condition for the possibility of believing and loving. It is open-ness to the light of faith and to the action of love. Hope is the capacity in each of us to be open to God's truth and love that are revealed in Word and Spirit. Hope is that in us which defines us as *homo viator*, as being on the way, open to some-thing new coming into being in us, to that which has hereto-fore been thought of as nearly impossible, beyond our imagining.

As a theological virtue, hope is at once a gift and our activity. We grow in hope precisely by being hopeful, by acting hopefully. Hope must be exercised, even in the face of what seems to be hopeless, and especially in the face of our own feelings of hopelessness.

Hope Endures

Does hope endure? Does hope remain after we breathe our last? Again, Rahner is helpful here. He begins by distinguishing theological hope from hope in and of itself, the fundamental human dynamic of hope. He wonders why there are traditionally three virtues when the mode of God's self-communication is two-fold. We are created with the capacity for self-transcendence through the two-fold mode of knowledge and love corresponding to God's two-fold self-communication in Word and Spirit. Consequently, Rahner does not recognize hope as a distinct, third theological virtue situated between faith and love. If not a distinct albeit oft-forgotten theological virtue between faith and love, what then is hope?

For Rahner, hope is the undergirding thrust, that drive by which we are always *in via*, on the way. Hope is a permanent disposition, the active underpinning of knowledge and love as openness to the unfathomable mystery of God through knowing and loving. But crucial to Rahner's understanding of hope is this: the God for whom we search and strive in all our knowing and loving cannot be possessed. Because the encounter with God through knowing and loving is salvific, and because salvation is ongoing and not already accomplished and so not something that can be possessed, hope as the enduring disposition toward the unfathomable mystery of God does not end.

This is a clear departure from the vast majority of articulations of hope by Catholic theologians. As but one example, for Thomas Aquinas hope does not abide in the Beatific Vision, because in the Beatific Vision what one hopes for is now possessed. Not only is this the understanding that colors the bulk of the Roman Catholic theological tradition, not surprisingly it is also the understanding of hope coursing throughout the body of spiritual and mystical writings in the tradition. Put starkly: hope ends at death.

Rahner's insight, put in very simple terms, is that our faith is *in* God known as Father, Son/Word, and Spirit. The love of God is expressed through our love *of* neighbor. But the nature of hope is different. Hope is more immediate, more direct in the human person's relationship with God. Hope is more basic, more fundamental. Whereas faith is *in* God and love is *of* God and *of* our neighbor, *hope hopes God.*

What becomes of hope when what I have affirmed in faith is no longer believable? What happens to hope when faith is shattered, when one's belief in beliefs crumbles? Without faith, how can hope be anchored? If the all-loving, all-knowing, all-powerful God is beyond belief in light of the enormity of human suffering and pain, is hope in God to be jettisoned along with the tattered and shattered belief in such a God?

Taking a cue once more from Rahner, hope remains even when the "what" or "whom" of our belief is no longer believed, or even when we feel no longer able to love the object or recipient of our love. Even then hope remains.

It is precisely in the weakness of faith, even in the loss of faith, that we uncover the deepest meaning of hope. The deepest kind of hope goes on hoping precisely when there is no

consolation to be drawn from it. Real hope does not constantly look for assurances of God's nearness, nor does hope try to
determine how God's providence will be made being manifest
in one's life, in the lives of others, or in the world at large.
Hope may even take the form of challenging traditional expla-
nations of God's will. By hope we navigate through the mis-
take of taking hiddenness and silence for the non-existence of
God. Hope remains open to all new and often astonishing
manifestations of the divine life, even the presence of God that
may be known in the experience of absence or utter darkness.
It is only hope that clings to God after God is gone from us—
or is it rather we who are gone from God? Hope knows that
after God there is nothing but God.

Hope beyond Death

What, then, of hope beyond the grave? It remains. Following
Rahner in his departure from Thomas Aquinas and the main-
stream of the Catholic tradition, we see that whatever the
afterlife may be in terms of states in life, there will be hope.
Extending Rahner's insight further, even those who do not as
yet enjoy what is thought of as heavenly bliss continue to
hope. And it is this hope—enduring still among the dead—
that is an openness to God's reach, to Christ's descent even
into the bottoms, to the netherworld.

The difference between Rahner and Aquinas on the enduring character of hope should not be overdrawn. In responding
to the question of whether the suffering of those in purgatory
is voluntary, Aquinas maintains that their suffering is voluntary, for if they did not know that they would be set free, they
would not ask for prayers, as they often do. This suggests that

souls "in between" do indeed hope, or else they would not ask for the prayers of the living.

Further, careful reading of Aquinas on the sacraments yields a more nuanced understanding of hope at and beyond death. Recall that the sacrament of the Eucharist is the principal sacrament of healing and transformation. In his *Commentary on Book IV of the Sentences*, Aquinas describes the *res* (the ultimate reality signified) of the sacrament of the Eucharist as *transformatio hominis in Deum* (transformation of human beings into God). *Deum* is in the accusative, implying "motion" or "ongoing" (dynamic), as opposed to the ablative *Deo*, which would imply rest or place (static). Using *in* followed by the accusative leaves room for growth for us after death, growth that will never end, whereas using *in* followed by the ablative seems to suggest that the Beatific Vision will be full and complete from the start, so that there is no room for further growth in participation in the inner life of God.

As the last of the sacraments received by the Christian at death, the Eucharist is understood as *viaticum*, that is, provision for the journey. In other words, the end of the Eucharist is the *ongoing* divinization of human beings, even in dying and at death.

Often thought to be an irrelevant residual insight from the long ago, the Christian belief in purgatory offers insight here. Just as heaven is not a geographical place up there or out there, hell does not have an address in the bowels of the earth. And purgatory is not a waiting room in between. Rather, these three terms are ways of describing states of the soul. And we experience all three proleptically, or in the manner of anticipation, in the course of our lives. We taste heaven, purgatory, and hell already here on earth, but not yet fully. This is expressed when we hear someone say, after listening to Handel's *Messiah* or Barber's *Adagio for Strings*, that the performance was heavenly. When people are in anguish, be it physical or mental, they say their experience is like a living hell. When living close to someone who is annoying or irritable or worse, we might say that we are doing our purgatory here on earth. In more traditional language, we have a foretaste of each while we dwell on earth.

Even though the finality of death is sure, and dying is not something we experience in part, there is insight from other epochs and cultures that provides a more nuanced understanding of what becomes of us after death. Death is not a terminus at which we finally arrive. There may indeed be movement and activity that does not end when we take our last breath.

HEAVEN

In that state of soul called heaven, we continue to grow in knowledge and love propelled by hope in what is yet more, the unfathomable mystery called God who always eludes our grasp. Heaven is the dimension of openness to God, where God dwells, where God's presence is discerned, where God may be said to be known and loved, albeit still incompletely. For it is in the nature of God to be incomprehensible mystery. And it is in the nature of the human person to move in hope toward ever deeper knowing and loving. If the desire for knowing and loving cease, then it is no longer really I who have been saved in the salvific encounter with God in truth and love. The quest for deeper truth and love is who I am. I not only have questions. I am a question. What is more: I quest both here and beyond. And still beyond.

PURGATORY

At the moment of our death, most of us are not finished. We have in various ways squandered God's gift, have failed in manifold ways to make good on the one and only life God has given us. All the growth and development that has taken place over the course of our lives is incomplete.

In purgatory, movement continues but, in a manner of speaking, the distance we must traverse is greater because we have in manifold ways misused and betrayed the gifts given by God in Word and Spirit, and so growth in truth and love is more arduous and cannot be accomplished at once. Nor do I grow in knowledge and love alone. Hence the longstanding practice of praying for the souls in purgatory. There is life there. And hope. Further, some recent theological reflection yields the insight that the dead are not only the beneficiaries of our prayer, but they too are active in the ongoing work of salvation by their endeavor to forgive those with whom they lived while dwelling among mortals. Thus their participation in the ongoing salvation of the world continues.

Whatever is to be said of activity beyond the grave, purgation or purgatory is God's act. Again, recall that whatever is meant by purgation as God's act, this takes place outside time and space in an altogether different universe than the one we mortals inhabit. In an exercise of the eschatological imagination, this can be spoken of only in the way of approximation, that is, in language that is inexact because of the nature of the reality it seeks to express: living beyond death.

As God's act beyond our dying and death, purgation describes an intensity of transformation. At our death we are still in need of psychological healing. Different dimensions, or levels, of our self, what Thomas Merton called the "true self," are as yet unintegrated. Levels of our personality remain disordered and warped. The fullness of life is not yet ours. But it yet may be by God's own doing. Rather than a forbidding state, purgatory is a region of hope.

Again, in the language of approximation that is the speech of the eschatological imagination, what may be said of hell?

HELL

Week by week, we profess our faith in the communion of saints. The teaching church makes bold to say that Mary Magdalene, Teresa of Kolkata, Damien of Molokai, and John XXIII are in the thick of that blessed communion. But for all the talk in Christian churches about hell, even as Holy Mother Church carefully and sometimes haltingly names particular persons as saints in heaven, no human being has been named as one who has been cast into the eternal abyss of hell, the domain of Satan, and the region of those who are said by some to be lost and beyond hope for eternity.

In hearing this there is a tendency among some to detect a hint of the suggestion that the good and the bad, the sheep and the goats, the oppressed and their oppressors, meet the same end. This is then quickly followed by earnest questions about why one should bother to live a good and virtuous life, since in the end we all arrive at the same destination. To this there can only be one response: we are to strive to make good on the one and only life we have to live in response to what we know to be the irresistible draw of God's love. Not because of reward or punishment.

Those who followed Jesus while he lived among mortals did so because of the love he embodied. Indeed, he reminded his followers to set aside preoccupations about who among them would be first in the kingdom, which is to say, how they might be rewarded. And so it is to be with those who have been baptized into his Body, following him generation after generation, those who have gone before us, and those of us mortals still dwelling on the earth.

As mentioned earlier, while the church affirms the doctrine of the communion of saints and names particular persons who are said to be with God in heaven, the church has never pronounced by name that this or that human person is in hell. Hell is the domain of Satan, who may be said to be a power, but not a human person. We have no sound basis on which to stake the claim that this or that person is in Satan's grip for all eternity.

Some earlier approaches to catechesis would single out particular human beings as most certainly among those burning in hell. In religious instruction during the years immediately following World War II, Adolf Hitler was said to be burning in the scorching fires of hell alongside Judas the Betrayer and Luther the Reformer! While such assertions may have been well intentioned, they were most certainly misguided.

There is no doubt that human beings fail to make good on the life they have been given, and that they do indeed harm one other and inflict pain and bring destruction to nations, races, classes, cultures, and whole peoples. How are we to judge such failure, such outright betrayal of the gift given, in light of the mercy of God beyond measure, a mercy that does not erase the requirements of justice in its bestowal?

In his encyclical *Spe salvi*, Benedict XVI offers insight on the nature of Christian hope. Given the challenges to hope in our age, especially the widespread injustice that renders life nearly impossible for millions, he identifies three "settings" for learning and practicing hope: prayer, action and suffering, and the final judgment (32–48). It is the last of these that throws light on a proper understanding of heaven, purgatory, and hell.

For Benedict, the image of the Last Judgment has all but faded from the contemporary mind. The last, or general, final judgment, according to Benedict, is not an image of terror, but of hope. According to Benedict, for the Christian, it may be the defining image of hope, because apart from what awaits each of us individually at the hour of our death there is, in the end, a final reckoning when both justice and mercy will prevail.

Benedict speaks in nuanced language of profiles and types of people who "could" be in hell. That there "can be" people who cut themselves off from truth and love irrevocably indicates that hell can exist. But it exists as a possibility. There is, then, the possibility that one could reach a point of complete alienation from God through arrogance and opulence, domination and self-indulgence, destruction of innocent life and willful acts of oppression and injustice. But between death and resurrection, the defining judgment of the soul that is often said to be irreversible or beyond remedy has not yet become final.

The image of the Last Judgment reminds us that grace does not cancel out justice. It does not make wrong right. It is not a sponge that wipes everything all away so that what we and others have done on earth ends up being of equal value or morally neutral. But nowhere in his treatment does Benedict speak of being cast into the fires of hell as God's punishment. Rather, he speaks of hell as the state of soul of those who, by their own doing, have totally destroyed their desire for truth and their readiness to love. Careful to avoid identifying anyone by name as being in such a state, he makes a non-specific reference to alarming profiles of this type of person from the bygone century. But these are types that would fit the description of individuals who have destroyed their desire for truth and readiness to love. Critically important here is that in speaking ever so briefly of hell, the governing concern of Benedict is with justice, not individual punishment, setting right the wrong that has been done by acts of oppression and injustice that make victims of millions.

In much more helpful imagery than that of fiery flames, Benedict uses a very evocative image borrowed from Dostoyevsky in his effort to express the meaning of purgatory and hell. Evildoers in the end do not sit at the same table in the eternal banquet beside their victims without distinction, as if nothing has happened. If the state of the soul is thought of in terms of place, those in hell, purgatory, and heaven will not all be in the same place in the banquet hall. Taking the image a step further, some may be seated at a distance from the banquet table, while others are at tables still farther away. And some may be in the corridors outside the banquet hall, waiting and hoping that there might yet be room enough for them.

Likewise, Benedict offers an alternative image of heaven, what he calls the known unknown. Heaven, being with God for all eternity, is not to be thought of as a never-ending succession of uninterrupted blissful days. Benedict goes so far as to say that heaven, thus understood, would be boring. Rather, heaven is better thought of as a supreme moment of satisfaction, something akin to plunging into an ocean of infinite love.

It is clear in the Christian tradition that at the moment of our death, our life choice which over the course of our lifetime has taken a certain direction becomes definitive in the sense that it defines who I am before God in the moment of my

death. But is it final? And, if so, why distinguish between particular judgment at my death and the general, or last, judgment of all?

The judgment at death may be thought of as defining, but
in a manner that may leave room for growth and even change.
In this sense, the judgment at death defines who I am before
God at that moment. But it is still pending, or is deferred, until
the final judgment is rendered.

The final judgment as an image of hope, not terror, serves
as a reminder that there is an intermediate state between death
and resurrection, a state wherein there is yet to be an irrevoca-
ble judgment. Heaven and hell in their fullness are ushered in
only at the Last Judgment.

The distinction between the judgment at my death and the
Last Judgment has profound implications for Christian living.
It is anything but pie-in-the-sky speculation, for when I die
history continues. My death does not signal the end of the
world! Though I may have passed to another universe, what I
have done in this life—for good or ill—has yet to be realized in
its fullness. We now know that the butterfly flapping its wings
over the Pacific Ocean has some effect on the flow of water
through the Bering Strait. These days children are urged to go
potty before going swimming—even in the big and wide
Atlantic Ocean—because some of their parents are keenly
aware that toxins in the surf in Atlantic City may have a poi-
sonous effect on the fish in the South China Sea.

In similar, or approximate, fashion: everything I have
done in this life has bearing on human life, history, and the
world long after I breathe my last. The consequences of my
actions remain in the rest of human history and its making.
This is a loud and firm wakeup call to each and every one of

us to consider the ethical implications of each and every one of our actions.

The work of Jesus Christ is finished. His life, ministry, passion, dying, death, descent, and being raised to new life have already occurred. But the Christ event continues. In other words, the effects of what he has done are still at work, still present and active in human life, history, the world, and the church. The same applies to what we have done and what we have failed to do.

Thus it may be said that at our death the verdict remains pending. The jury is still out until the last day. It is at the Last Judgment that judgment will be final, at that time beyond all time when the effects of what we have done—for good or ill—and their impact on the cosmos will be made manifest, that "moment" when the power of love prevails over all evil and every tear is wiped away.

Can there be change or activity after death? Can there be movement—even conversion—after death? These are slippery questions. They should not cause us to lose sight of the distinction between judgment at death and the final judgment. This distinction makes room enough for the inexhaustible love of God that reaches out to all the dead, indeed, even to those thought deserving of eternal punishment in a hell that would not even be as a possibility were it not for the love of God—refused.

That Christ descends, gathering everyone and everything into the bosom of Divine Love, may smack of universal salvation. However, it is rather more expressive of the deepest kind of hope and confidence in the mercy of God beyond calculation, for God's justice is both gracious and merciful. The descent to the dead is not only an event of the past. By God's ongoing self-communication its effects continue through time to subsequent generations. This serves as an indication that, at least as a possibility, all may be saved. Life beyond the grave is a continuation of life on earth. We cannot repair the evil we have done. Nor can we initiate good actions—on our own. But as in life so in death we can pray, asking Christ for forgiveness, healing, and help for ourselves and others. Christ is with the dead, not in the sense that death is final, but in the sense that the dead are with him on the way to fuller participation in the unfathomable mystery, plunging more deeply into the ocean of love that knows no bounds.

For both Karl Rahner and Hans Urs von Balthasar, hell exists as a possibility. They maintain the possibility of eternal loss for every individual, for each one of us, because otherwise human freedom and the shaping of human history would be rendered insignificant. The possibility that freedom will end in eternal loss stands alongside the Christian conviction that the world and the history of the world as a whole will in fact enter into eternal life with God, that is, heaven. Hell is thus a necessary, logical possibility, but not a certain reality.

If hell exists as a possibility, dare we imagine that it might be possible that Christ, the medicine of life, bears a balm for our wounds even there? It is only the deepest kind of hope that endures all things, that is open to even such a possibility, which can only come as a gift. Might we dare hope for the possibility of the non-existence of hell?

Here we recall that what was first affirmed in the faith of the church was that Christ descended to the dead rather than into hell. Some have referred to Ephesians 4:9, which tells of Christ descending to "the lower regions of the earth." The first letter of Peter 3:19–20 has been frequently used as a scriptural foundation for the belief in the descent in its affirmation that "he went to speak to the spirits in prison."

In the story of Noah, it was only a few, eight in all, who escaped in the ark through the waters. The vast number of mortals were outside the ark. Might we dare hope that in Christ's generous descent, God's incarnate love does not forget those outside the ark? After all, God's reach extends beyond the ark. Perhaps beyond the ark of the covenant. And perhaps even beyond our understandings of the new covenant in Christ's blood. For his body was given and his blood spilled so that they might have life and have it to the full—they, perhaps meaning even and especially those among the living who may be drowning in the waters beyond the ark, imprisoned in the circles of suffering that make of their lives a living hell.

CHAPTER 8

The Immensity of Saturday

THE CHRISTIAN FAITH is lived where we are, in the time in which we live. The present age is defined for us by terrible memories, by war, by disease, by massive injustice, by fears for the future. The very hopes of building a new world order—hopes entertained by humanity and especially Western countries in the nineteenth and twentieth centuries—have been confounded by memories of two world wars and untold numbers of local wars, of the Holocaust of the Jewish people and other genocides still under way, of famines and epidemics left uncontrolled, and at present by a breakdown of international organizations intended to foster peace and human flourishing. Networks of nations are dissolving in the face of claims to military power and the righteousness of peoples. God's name is invoked in justifying terrorism and punitive onslaught. The summons to peace and justice issued by both church and nations has little claim on those who are determined to bring about order amidst the chaos or, more accurately, what they judge to be the right order of things.

The church is in a very different position to that in which it was a hundred or even fifty years ago. In many respects, it is no longer a central figure on the world stage. Its voice has become weakened. It has become weakened internally by failure to live according to the testimony of Christ and by some reverberating scandals. It has become weakened externally by reason of other plausible claims to truth, even and especially on the part of those made by some currents of secularity that could enrich the human quest for a new and better world order but that are dismissed outright as evils of "secularism," a term at once slippery and capacious. Despite its past strong claims to being the source of truth, it is now called to open its heart and its mind to others and to other religions, to purify its own memories, and, perhaps above all, to internal spiritual and institutional reform. How in these times may it find a voice to speak the words of God and of Jesus Christ, Son and Word of the Father? And how is it to capture and spread anew the light of Christ in this, our own very dark age?

The distress and suffering in the wider world are echoed in our own personal lives. Or is it rather that the darkness of our own lives, dwelling as so many do in the circles of suffering and death, is made manifest and multiplied in the hell on earth that is swallowing so many alive? The mounting number of suicides among the young and the dramatic rise in the number of people of all ages suffering from major depression are just two indicators of the depth of darkness in which so many are caught. There seems to be no way forward. How to find the voice of God when faced with the inconsolable sorrow of a mother who has given birth to a baby affected by the Zika virus? What light does the gospel of Jesus Christ bring to the scene in which a husband has just learned from his wife of the onset of early illness that will take her life? And how do we begin to make a way forward in the face of the suffocation, the strangulation, of Mother Earth, our common home?

Ours may be said to be a Holy Saturday society. Holy Saturday connotes rupture and termination; a sense of darkness and disintegration; the loss of meaning, hope, and creativity. The state of the world in which we live evokes a pervasive anxiety, a widespread fear and despair. Waking up in the morning to the news of yet of another terrorist attack; realizing that we enter into wars that appear to have no clear or justifiable purpose and never seem to end; listening to politicians whose speech is marked by acrimonious and violent language...at such moments it may seem that the whole world has descended into hell. If we are honest with ourselves, there are times when the resurrection doesn't seem real.

Those who are alert are witnesses to the expiration of whole peoples and cultures. There is an omnipresent skepticism, fear, and fanaticism. There is the rise of religious extremism of all sorts. And so the conviction that Christ has shared our hell speaks not only to one's personal hell, but might also offer solace to those millions entrapped in the many circles of hell in our own day.

Alleluia! Is that so? The words ring hollow for so many. How do we ring out joy even as we are aware of the millions who live in the circles of suffering, and so many of us and those we love seem to be caught in hell's grip?

We are in the throes, wittingly or not, of our own demise. Without the story of God's descent into the immensity, the depth that is beyond measure, of all that Saturday means, how could we hope? Does the gospel speak in a credible way to those communities and peoples clenched in the jaws of death even as they dwell among the living?

We look to vital forces that spring from this "dead symbol," the Christ interred who descends to the dead, so that it might offer both comfort and hope to those persons and communities, nations, races, and classes living in the shadow of death. This is possible only when the narrative of the three days is read and heard rightly.

The narrative of the three days must be read and heard first and foremost with new eyes and ears, forward from the Thursday evening through to the Sunday morning. The story needs to be read forward first, and only then backward; then again from beginning to end. We allow the text to be revelatory when we do not read the text in light of its conclusion with the resurrection on the third day. When read in proper sequence, the gospel accounts suggest that the disciples experienced despair and darkness at the death of Christ. For them, this death was not a partial experience, assuaged by intuitions that on the third day the stone would be rolled away and Mary of Magdala would run to Peter and the other disciples and tell them what she saw or, true to the text, what she heard. The starkness of the death of Jesus is glossed over in our reading and hearing because the events of the Friday, Saturday, and Sunday are interpreted primarily, if not exclusively, in view of the resurrection on the third day. But this is the Paschal Mystery proclaimed and heard backwards, from the Sunday morning looking back. Far too often the events of Jesus' final days and hours are proclaimed and heard in such a way that the end of the plot is already known. But we can understand this text as revelatory only if we enter into it at the beginning.

Even though all analogies limp to greater or lesser degree, consider the way we read a poem. We do not begin reading from the last line to the first. We start at the beginning and read through to the last line. It is only then that we may go back over this or that line to see how the beauty of each line fits into the whole. Or, to use a different example, reading a mystery novel while knowing the resolution from the start defeats the very point of reading the story.

We begin at the beginning. We have known, in our own lives and in the lives of others, the experience of the Friday: moments of excruciating pain, loss, anguish, betrayal, loneliness, darkness. And we know moments of the Sunday: delight, bliss, surprise, vigor, rejuvenation, hope. But what is it to know that moment of the Paschal Mystery marked by the Saturday when the love of God in Christ went to the netherworld, to the bottoms, among the dead, into hell?

Just as nothing much happens during the Sacred Triduum on Holy Saturday, the Saturday of Christ's descent is a space of liminality, those "existential margins" wherein live those who are disillusioned, disappointed, those whose grip on life is tenuous, whose emptiness of stomach and spirit echoes in the ache of absence. If the gospel is to be received today as good news, then it is to be proclaimed in a way that springs from the silence and the sorrow of the Saturday. Friday marks the end of a life. On Sunday life begins anew.

But before the trumpets and the Alleluias, the shouts of victory and jubilation, we must wait, pause, ponder, attending to the generous descent of divine life in the most unlikely of persons and places. On the Saturday we wait. Hush. Still.

This liminality, this aching waiting, is central to the proclamation of the good news in our day. By becoming a Holy Saturday people, the church might give some small witness that here in Christ's tomb it is possible to find the confidence in a hopeful future—for those living at the existential peripheries, between the cracks of church and society, those who are unloved, abandoned, and forgotten. Living the mystery of

Holy Saturday day in and day out summons one to live the good news in the face of suffering, in the pain of darkness experienced by so many in the absence of hope, amidst the ravages of injustice as these are known in one's own life but more so in the lives of the faceless millions caught this day in the grip of suffering, in the circles of hell on earth. It is to live in the confidence that God's reach is deep enough, that *gratia sanans*, the healing grace of the Word and the Spirit, is strong enough to withstand, endure, and prevail over the power of evil—unto death and into hell. It is to know that Christ's descent to the dead is at once the endpoint of the *kenosis* as well as the first moment of his exaltation.

Between Friday's cry of abandonment and surrender and Sunday's victory over death and glorification lies the Saturday. Holy Saturday, the Saturday of Glory. Before the trumpets and the Alleluias, the shouts of victory and jubilation, we must wait, pause, ponder, attending to the generous descent of divine life in mortal flesh. On the Saturday all our doings, projects, plans, accomplishments, and achievements lie fallow. Wait. Still. Waiting.

In the silence of the Saturday we can hear and tell the story at the second day, the seventh day. Hearing the good news as if for the first time we must pause here and dwell in the silence. It is only by attending to the mystery of the death and descent of God in Christ in all its staggering starkness that we can be still enough to hear the stirring of the impossible possibility: the love that is shown in the power of God's weakness in dying and death does not die. There is still God, in the tomb, a God whose presence is known in absence.

Christ's descent on the seventh day, the time of Sabbath rest for the Jews, Holy Saturday for Christians, is the bolt that holds together the Paschal Mystery. Theology and practice meet on Holy Saturday. God's presence in the tomb is the very foundation of Christian hope. From this all other elements of Christian life in the Spirit emerge and are given their proper direction.

Christian theology and spirituality are two dimensions of the quest for an answer to the question which Jesus himself asked as he was dying. Jesus' cry from the cross is expressive of his solidarity with all human suffering and death. As he bore our nature as living, he bore our nature as dead.

While his views of the Paschal Mystery are the subject of ongoing theological discussion, Hans Urs von Balthasar's insights are crucial to understanding the mystery of Christ's descent. In this view, the cross is a Trinitarian event. Jesus, Son and Word, dies forsaken by the one he called Father. In his dying, Jesus enters into "godforsakeness." And the Father knows "sonlessness." The cross afflicts not only the Son, but the Three in One Love, the God whose very being is to be in loving relation. This is to say that in the very life of the Triune God, there is travail, real suffering. The Father suffers from the loss of the Son as the Son suffers from death and abandonment by the Father. The cross signals a rupture of their communion in the One Love. Critically important, even here as we speak of the death of Jesus, Son and Word, is that death is never a partial experience.

Godlessness is existence in hell. It is the state of soul in which one is estranged or separated from God. To live in the hope of the resurrection it is utterly imperative that nothing of the "godforsakeness" of the Son and "sonlessness" of the Father is canceled out—or even ever so slightly muted. The

Father's "yes" to Jesus in no way erases the deadly hellishness of all that the Father and the Son endured.

If the church is to give testimony to the truth of the original proclamation of the good news—the Crucified One lives—amidst the circles of suffering and the grip of hell in which millions live, its witness will ring hollow unless and until Christians identify as Christ did, not only with the joys and hopes, but more so with the ruptures and sorrows and, yes, the expiration of the values, language, sense of belonging, and culture—what Jürgen Habermas calls the "lifeworld"—of a people threatened especially by the negative forces of globalization, to say nothing of the violations of Mother Earth caused by unbridled want and greed.

If indeed the descent is the linchpin of the good news, the bolt that holds together the Paschal Mystery, then the Christian and the Christian people are summoned to share more deeply in the world's suffering, godforsakeness, dying, and death as a participation in Jesus' godforsakeness and the Father's sonlessness known in the interruption of their communion in the One Love.

Imprisoned by the Gestapo during the Second World War, Dietrich Bonhoeffer wrote: "Only a suffering God can help." No matter how excruciating my suffering, no matter how unspeakable the pain of a person or a people, Christ has also known such horror. And there is hope for us because he himself has been delivered from the hands of Hades. Only if Jesus is truly human in suffering, dying, death, and descent can we affirm a true resurrection of the dead.

While it does not rank high in the church's hierarchy of truths, the descent may be thought of as the sleeping center of

Christian faith and life. Without the doctrine of Christ's descent to the dead, into hell, Christian faith in an incarnate and crucified Son of the Father who is raised to new life is implausible in the face of the hellish suffering of millions. It is in faith and praxis rooted in Christ's descent into all that the seventh day—Holy Saturday—means that the church has something to offer the world. The gospel cannot be proclaimed in its fullness without the descent. Without it, how can anyone believe in the good news of Jesus Christ as either good or news? For us and for our salvation not only did Jesus die and rise but also descended to the dead. If the descent is blotted out from our memory, if it is ignored in the church's preaching and catechesis, if it remains in the dustbin of theological reflection, how can we possibly offer hope to the world? Proclaiming and singing Alleluias alone is a failure to give testimony to the good news that it is the Crucified One, dead and buried, who descended among the dead, who lives!

Even though for some Christ's descent may not be understood as part of the apostolic witness, the church has affirmed the descent in its believing bones from the very beginning. *Lex orandi, lex credendi*—what the church prays is what the church believes.

Consider the Sacred Triduum, the high point of the church's liturgical year, the apex of its communal prayer. This consists of three days, with days understood to begin at sundown. On Holy Thursday evening we celebrate the Eucharist, mindful in a particular way of the Lord's Last Supper on the night before he died. This is done with great solemnity, as is the somber celebration of Good Friday. Together with the reading of the Lord's Passion, there is also the exaltation and veneration of the cross on the Friday. But then there is no Mass until the

Easter Vigil and the Day Mass of Easter on the third day of the Triduum. What, then, of Holy Saturday? From ancient times there has been no communal Eucharist, thereby marking not only Christ's interment but also his descent among the dead. From early on there was only silence on that day.

Some consider the absence of Mass to mark Holy Saturday as itself indicative of the minor—some might say insignificant—role of the descent in the life and prayer of the church. But is it possible that entering the blank space, the point of pause and poise between cross and resurrection, will make it possible for the church to find its true identity with the one who between the times of the first and third days was among the dead? More: perhaps it is because we do not bring to voice the desolation, the aloneness, the abandonment, the forgotteness experienced by so many today—signaled in the dead Christ's corpse—that preaching and teaching seem to throw little or no light on the lived reality of the Christian people.

In the first story of creation (Genesis 1:1–31; 2:1–4), on the seventh day after the heavens and the earth and all their array were completed, God rested. On the seventh day of the week, the Lord's Day, the people of the covenant keep the Sabbath holy by refraining from work and everyday activities (Exodus 20:8–10). They stop. They gather. They pray. They rest. It is the day of quiet repose and recollection.

In the traditions of both Jews and Christians, the number seven is richly layered in meaning. That Jesus instituted the seven sacraments in the strict and formal sense is the subject of ongoing discussion among sacramental theologians and liturgists. But that for the last several centuries these are numbered seven is certain. And the numbering is not arbitrary.

For Christian people, the day of rest, the Sabbath, is not the seventh day but the first day of the week, the Sunday. It was on this first day of the week that the bold proclamation first reached the ears of the followers of Jesus of Nazareth: The Crucified One lives! But this should not obscure the fact that Jesus was crucified before sundown on the sixth day, the Friday, so that he could be buried before the Sabbath, the seventh day, so that all, even those who stood by him until the end, could stop, rest, and pray.

In some of the Eastern Christian churches there are liturgical celebrations that commemorate Christ's entombment, that period between the Friday and the Sunday when he lay dead. But in the liturgical life of the Western church, Holy Saturday may seem like a long, gaping pause. Not much happens in the church between the Friday and the Sunday. This second day is a bit ambiguous. It is a brief, slender, unnoticed, and seemingly insignificant dimension of Christ's Pasch. But if we are to share in the fullness of Christ's Pasch, we must enter at this ambiguous and invisible boundary between the Friday and the Sunday.

Rather than the Saturday being a time to catch our breath between Holy Thursday, Good Friday, and the preparation of the festive dinner on Easter Sunday, Holy Saturday, the seventh day, is properly understood as a time of silence, a time of pondering the mystery of God's presence in absence, redoubling our efforts to be vigilant in the face of the tendency to treat Christ's death as a partial participation in human existence. Indeed, Christ—the whole Christ, not just this or that side or part of him—is interred, descends into the place of the dead, announcing the good news that death is no more. The most appropriate response is an awe-inspired silence as the very life, light, and love of God in Christ goes to the bottoms as a fellow dead man to be with, to comfort, and to bring good news even to those who have died.

In Spanish Holy Saturday is sometimes rendered *Sabado de Gloria*, which is so much richer in significance than *Sabado Santo*. The Saturday of Glory is that time all ashimmer during which we anticipate the fulfillment of our hopes, rather than a liturgical lacuna between Good Friday and Easter. Saturday, the seventh day, is a time of silence, a space for pondering the mystery of God with us as the God whose presence is known in absence.

As we have already seen, the immutable, impassible God, rooted in classical metaphysical theology, cannot adequately address let alone answer questions about the world's suffering. But this is not the God we encounter on the cross or in the tomb. The God of Christian faith known in Jesus' incarnation and interment is no stranger to godforsakeness and sonlessness. The rupture and disintegration, indeed the immense suffering characteristic of our Holy Saturday society, is now at the very heart of the Divine Trinity. And God is no less God for it. We who are to give flesh to this mystery do so in word and deed as a Holy Saturday people in a Holy Saturday world: In death God never ceases to be God.

There is no possibility for us, creation, or the cosmos that is beyond the reach of the Three in One Love, Whose love is unquenchable, unfathomable, inexhaustible mystery. No one who has passed, no one who passes away, is past because the immensity of God's reach knows no bounds.

CHAPTER 9

Living into Saturday

DISTINCT CHRISTIAN SPIRITUALITIES arise in response to the Spirit at work in human life, history, the world, and the church. The Spirit, the very life of God dwelling within us, is at work within different cultures at particular times and in specific places, in efforts to interpret and live within tradition, in the struggle to combine elements of prayer and action, and in discerning gifts bestowed for the service of community.

Any particular Christian spirituality, be it called Ignatian, Franciscan, that of the communities of l'Arche of Jean Vanier or the Focolare Movement, is properly understood as the Spirit-assisted response to live the gospel in earnest in view of contemporary needs and exigencies often emerging due to cultural upheaval or historical shifts. A Franciscan spirituality is no more or less than the effort of Giovanni Bernardone and Chiara Offreduccio, known as Francis and Clare of Assisi, to live the gospel *sine glossa*, that is, without compromise, within the culture of their time. The surge of urbanization in their day resulted in masses of poor people moving from countryside to village to city. The followers of Francis and Clare sought to follow the poor Christ in ways of life particularly suited to the shifting modes of perceiving and being during the age in which they lived.

Any particular spirituality is shaped in no small measure by the way in which Jesus Christ is remembered, the predominant image of Christ at work in a person or community.

Faced with what was understood as an aberration of the Christian faith among the Albigensians in the south of France, Dominic Guzman recognized in Christ the preacher and teacher the way to the truth. His singular focus on the preaching and teaching Christ gave rise to a school, or approach, to spirituality that bears his name and is lived preeminently in the members of the Order of Preachers he founded.

Awash in the destruction and division wrought by the Second World War, Chiara Lubich heard the cry of Jesus abandoned and forsaken on the cross as a summons to work for the reconciliation of all peoples. This gave birth to the Focolare Movement, whose members devote their lives—in different ways and walks of life—to the unity of peoples in the church and the wider world.

Exposed to the poverty of so many in the streets of Kolkata, the most recent Teresa to be inscribed in the book of saints found hope in the depths of her own darkness as she looked on Christ Crucified and heard his words, "I thirst." In each of the houses of the Missionaries of Charity, the religious community she founded, hangs a crucifix with the words of Jesus: "I thirst." This signifies not only the hunger and thirst of the poor, abandoned, and forgotten in the Body of Christ, but also Christ's thirst for each one of the Missionaries of Charity.

Each of these images emerges from and gives shape to a way of living the gospel in response to shifting perceptions and particular needs.

What is the understanding of Christ most apt for our own time and place? What is the way of discipleship most suited to the incarnation of the gospel today? Who is this Christ we follow? Where is the call of Christ to be heard, and how are we to follow? The answer to these questions may seem obvious unless and until we recognize that we do not yet know fully who Christ is and, in seeking to understand him, there is always more and yet more again to know and to love as we respond to his grace in the here and now of our own time and place. We shall not know fully who Christ is until the power of love prevails over all evil and Christ is all in all.

We ask: Where is God to be found in the immensity of Saturday? How far are we to follow? And we are brought to the edge, to the peripheries of society and church. While *kenosis* bespeaks the mystery of God's self-emptying love in the midst of our brokenness, our wounds, our failures, it is Christ's *descent* that brings *kenosis* to the endpoint that reveals the presence of God's light, life, and love when we are laid low, so low that there is no lower to go. In Christ's generous descent, the love of God comes to us when we are utterly and absolutely lost, when there are no familiar markers to guide us in our efforts to find some good in the face of evil, bringing some truth amidst collapsing cultures built on the illusion of self-satisfaction, self-determination, and self-sufficiency, and offering a shimmering glimmer of beauty in the midst of the perversions of our own doing and the horrors of our own making.

What are the contours of a Christian spirituality when it is shaped in a defining way by Christ's descent—the culmination of kenotic humiliation and the first stirring of glorification? What might we do to carry and keep alive the spirit of the Saturday even as we live in the fullness of Sunday's new life?

An Act of/Active Hope

As the history of Christian spirituality has often shown, the risk in any approach to the spiritual life is that it may become overly self-focused and individualistic, a personal, indeed private, approach to self-perfection through life of prayer and the pursuit of virtue.

Hope is the openness to possibility that comes only as gift. What comes as gift is not of our doing, of our own efforts. Hope lies in waiting, enduring, anticipating. But there is more to hope, to hoping. Hope is a virtue and, as such, it is an action, an activity. That Christian hope is a divine gift that makes our relationship with God possible does not lessen the active nature of hope. We become hopeful by acting hopefully. The contemporary American poet Mary Oliver writes that faith is "tensile and cool." Perhaps too confident and self-assured? Smug? By contrast, hope is "a fighter and a screamer."

Attention was earlier drawn to those existential peripheries, the places or spaces of darkness in our own lives that we consciously or unconsciously push to the edges of our consciousness. They often erupt in anger, in rage, in violence to those we love and those who love us.

But the existential peripheries as described by Pope Francis are, in the first instance, those human conditions that keep millions from the fullness of human flourishing, those injustices and inequities that push people and whole peoples to the edges, to the margins: misery, ignorance, hunger, disease, malnutrition. Then there is the violence of war, or city streets, or of human trafficking. Why rehearse an inexhaustible list of unspeakable suffering and horrors beyond naming that keep millions in the circles of a living hell, among the living dead?

The surest hope of Christians is anchored in that "moment" in Christ's Pasch we know as the descent among the dead in which the love of God in Christ reaches to the farthest ends, the deepest depths, to those at the outermost margins, to those thought to be beyond all hope. In descending to the depths, the incarnate God brings light, life, and love to those in death. And also hope: death is no more!

A spirituality rooted in Christ's descent impels us to share in his mission of abolishing death and death dealing in our own time and place, not only in our personal lives and in the lives of those who are near, but even and especially in those who are trapped in the circles of unspeakable suffering, smothered and swallowed in the jaws of death at the existential peripheries.

Luminous Traces in the Dark

This approach to living the gospel calls us to a way of recognizing the presence of God in Christ and the quickening Spirit in the depths of human experience, at the bottoms, in that netherworld of darkness and death wherein there seems to be no hope, no light. The spiritual life is often envisaged in terms of ascent, of moving closer to God through various stages moving upward. This is charted out in the classical three ways in the spiritual life by which one moves upward from purgation to illumination to union with God at the apex. With roots in the writings of Church Fathers, theologians, and saints, this threefold framework charts the dynamic process, often very painful, by which one grows in virtue and sanctity. Through these three ways or stages, a person (1) is emptied of all that would keep one from God, (2) is given the light and grace to move more wholeheartedly toward God, and (3) loves God and others utterly and without limit. The movement is always onward and upward!

But the tradition also provides paths that urge us to recognize that God comes to us in our lowliness, when we are laid low, at the nadir.

Stages of prayer chart the dynamics of beginner, proficient, and perfect. We must always begin at the beginning. There is no other point of entry. Ignatius Loyola provides a manual of sorts in the *Spiritual Exercises* so that a wise guide can help the retreatant recognize the movements of grace in his or her life. But the movement of grace is rooted in Ignatius' principle and foundation, which requires that the retreatant recognize that he or she is a contingent being, a creature before the Creator. In his *Rule*, Benedict describes twelve steps of humility as the path to holiness. Even as the monk makes progress in this way, he is made constantly aware that God is the goal and humility is the way. And in the school of monastic wisdom, one often learns this the hard way by rubbing shoulders with others in community. The monk learns that the higher one moves up the ladder, the firmer must be the resolve to begin again at the bottom when one falls down flat on one's face.

The language of a spirituality from below, from the bottoms, from the dregs, finds most resonance perhaps with that life path known as the Twelve Steps. Much more than a program, this is a praxis involving the totality of oneself, the whole of one's life as one moves day by day from dependency to freedom. Originally Christian in inspiration, the language of the Steps was later reformulated so as to allow for the inclusion of those of all faiths, as well as those who profess no religious faith at all.

Some speculate that the Twelve Steps program is the most significant contribution the United States has made to the spiritual legacy of the twentieth century. This is arguable. But what is beyond dispute is that the Twelve Steps have healed, indeed saved, millions from the chains of dependency. The Twelve Steps do not work, however, or cannot be worked, unless and until one hits bottom, or "bottoms out." It is only when I accept that I am utterly powerless over that upon which I am dependent—be it alcohol, drugs, patterns of overeating, disordered sexual activity, gambling—that I can begin to move, or be moved, from the bottom.

One hurdle facing those in the bondage of dependency or addiction is that they never reach the bottom, or they are unable or unwilling to recognize that they really are already at the bottom. Some may lose friends, family, work, respect, health, or a future because of their dependency. Drink, drugs, overeating, sexual self-indulgence, or gambling are more important than anyone or anything else. There seems to be no bottom, or the bottom is bottomless.

The mystery of Christ's descent means that the love of God in Christ is reaching to heal, to soothe, to save—even and especially there, when I am free-falling to a bottom that knows no bottom. For God's love is without measure, beyond calculation. It knows no bounds. It does not count the cost of loving. And it is a persistent love that gets down on its knees, just like the woman searching every single corner and crevice of the house for her lost coin (Luke 15:8–10). But it goes yet farther, into the darkest and ugliest, indeed the most horrifying, corners of human existence to bring some small light, so that even the living dead might feel hope's pulse.

A spirituality rooted in Christ's descent stirs in us a recognition of God's love not only in the darkness and pain of our own deadly dregs, but also in those of others. Perhaps the greatest challenge after finding the seeds of the divine life in our own netherworld is that of accompanying others as they go deep into the netherworld of their own lives. But hardest of all is looking at the life of the one or ones we love who are living their mortal life in the prisons of hell of their own making. And then there are those millions who are living in the circles of suffering, their hellish lives made so not by themselves but by others who perpetrate systems of inequity and impoverishment. It is their voices we need to hear in Christ's cry, reminding us all that, as with Christ, suffering and death are not to be the defining words of their lives.

At times there is only a heart-rending silence in the face of the terrifying suffering that is visited upon so many. In the midst of the rubble and the ruin caused by yet another earthquake in Haiti, hands and voices were lifted to God in prayer and in praise. The Haitian people have given testimony time and again that they know that God is with them in their hellish tomb, is with them and comforts them and their beloved dead.

Others are so shackled by the effects of violence, hunger, and deprivation of all sorts that they are barely able to breathe. How dare we speak of God's unconditional love in the bottomless bottom of such suffering, to those who live each day in terror, whose every moment on the face of the earth is haunting and horrifying? Only in halting prayer that finds no words. At times there can be no more. It is the Saturday, the second day, the seventh day. When there is nothing to say, you say nothing.

At times we are able to lift our voice to God in lament, an oft-forgotten form of biblical prayer. We join our voice to Christ's as he cries to the Father, even when Abba does not seem to respond, appears to be doing nothing to come to our assistance. The love manifest in the death and descent of Christ is not power, but a blessed weakness. And at times we must recognize that there is little or nothing that can be done by those who have experienced their own powerlessness, and from there have been dragged from the dregs of darkness by God's soothing and saving grip alone.

FINDING GRACE IN THE GROTESQUE

A spirituality shaped by the descent is marked by its contemplative orientation. There remains a strong tendency to understand basic terms used to speak of Christian spirituality in very restricted ways, so that the "spiritual life" is thought to be concerned with interiority, recollection, self-perfection. "Prayer" is understood often as only something one does—either aloud or in silence—at specific times and places. And "contemplation" is thought to describe a very unusual, rarified kind of prayer that is practiced by the very few who are professed by vow in one of the canonical religious orders devoted to the "contemplative life."

Aware of the risk that comes with widening and opening up the meaning of these terms, we can say that "spirituality" refers to much more than the interior life or the practices of prayer. And "prayer" refers to more than what one does, often in quite wordy fashion, at specified times of the day or week. What is more, "contemplation" is not relegated to a designated few. Nor does the term refer only to one particular kind or movement of prayer. Contemplation is more properly understood as a whole way of being, a fundamental disposition of receptivity, the non-pragmatic regard for, or look toward, God, the other, others, and all creation. Contemplation or, better, contemplative living, is a way of seeing by loving and loving by seeing. The more I see, the more I love. The more I love, the more I see. This entails the lifelong discipline of learning how to see—how to read—the presence of God in human life, history, the wider world, and the church. It is for this reason that the Christian contemplative is often depicted with large, wide-open eyes. The contemplative is "all eyes," illumined by the light, vigilant so as to receive yet more of the light to see with the eyes of the heart.

"Heart" is the way we name the deepest or innermost self, the deep down self, the true self without pretending, without masks, without cover. The heart is a wide-open space wherein we glimpse, first and foremost, God's gaze upon us. In response, we search and stretch to know and be known, to love freely and be loved freely. It is here in this land of yearning for more and yet more and even still more again, this geography of desire, that God's Word and Spirit stir in us and evoke something in us, from us, for more than the self wants or desires—more and still more. In the course of our lifetime, this early, raw, sheer desire becomes more subtle. Through Word and Spirit it is purified, and thereby inclines to what is worthy of our desiring. In itself, desire is simply an indiscriminate wanting of it all. As it is gradually cleansed, the heart learns to long rightly. It comes to know what is good and true and beautiful by seeing with the eyes of the heart and so it desires only its own increase.

The heart is the seat of God's wisdom dwelling within. But the heart is also the region of our deepest wounds. Shaped by the mystery of Christ's descent, one who responds to the gift and task of living contemplatively must be vigilant so as to see and to receive. And what is seen, for those who have eyes to see in the darkness of Holy Saturday, is the shimmering in emptiness, the grace in the grotesque.

Beholding the Crucified One on the cross in our bedroom, or on the dashboard of the car, or dangling at the end of a Rosary, or lifted high over the altar of a church may move the heart to moments of prayerful recollection. Far too often we do not recognize that the cross signifies the whole world's "no" to Jesus, to his word and work, to his meaning and message. He dies a failure; the manner of his death, grotesque. Unless and until we are able to look on such grotesquery unflinchingly — a divine corpse in a tomb — we cannot truly rejoice in the Father's "yes" to the Crucified One by raising him to glory.

Looking to the mystery of Christ's descent, the contemplative sees the grace which is to be found in the grotesque, the unsightly, the ugly — indeed, sometimes in what is disgusting. It is not a pretty sight. Like the mentally disabled man whose body is disfigured and who needs constant care for his most basic needs. Or the frail, elderly woman whose body is racked with pain, who cannot walk, but who refuses to accept her diminishment and belligerently asserts that she needs no one. Or the violent massacre of innocents as an act of terror designed to get revenge and instill fear. Then there are the grotesque dimensions of our own lives: persistent impatience; an untamed acquisitive instinct that will never be content with what we have and have been given, but wants more and more and so takes it by hook or by crook; the harm we have knowingly done to others; our own complicity in the dysfunctional relationships between spouses, in our families, communities and, yes, in the church. Then there is our complicity in systems that depersonalize and dehumanize others, as well as in the unutterable horror of the suffocation of our mother, the earth.

None of this is to suggest that God's grace is to be found in acts of violence and terror, or in our inordinate efforts to get what we want, or in dysfunctional behavior. But it is to say boldly and unequivocally that, through the mystery of Christ's death and descent, the love of God reaches out, extends itself without limit or regard for the cost, so that it is always and everywhere on offer, even and especially amidst the most haunting and horrifying of human events, amidst the most grotesque of human experiences. Indeed the grotesquery of the crucifixion makes manifest a new measure of beauty: Love that gives itself in dying and death amidst violence, torture, hatred, mockery, injustice, and condemnation. It is in Christ's generous descent to the place of the dead, or into hell, that Love itself reaches and takes us in ways beyond our own doing, to that geography of hope and possibility which those living in death and its shadow are unable to see.

SAVING SALVE

This spirituality is rooted in an understanding of *gratia sanans*, the healing grace of Christ and the Spirit. Though they are not alone in this, the Syriac Fathers understood Christ's descent as the medicine of life. Christ bears the healing balm of the Spirit for our wounds. In understandings of salvation in Christ, it is often overlooked that the words "salvation" and "salve" are cognates. Salve, the ointment, or unction, or emollient that is applied to a wound, heals and protects. It restores to health what is hurt, broken, torn, or cut.

What does it mean when Christians affirm that salvation is through Christ, or that we are saved from sin by him? Sin is alienation or estrangement from God. Continuing in disordered relationships furthers sin's increase. Sin is a wound. Christ saves us by bearing the balm by which our alienation, estrangement, and woundedness are soothed and brought back to health so that we might live in right relationship with God, the other, others, every living creature, and all creation. Such salvation is accomplished in Christ's passion, suffering, dying, and death on the cross. But the descent brings this even further.

A medical practice from the not too distant past offers insight here. It is common practice these days that when sickness strikes and lingers we get ourselves one way or another to the urgent care clinic or to the emergency room, walking in accompanied or alone or, perhaps, taken by ambulance. But it was not so long ago that, when one was seriously ill and unable to get to the doctor, that doctor would make a "house call." Everyone knew that the doctor's time was precious and that house calls were above and beyond the call of the doctor's duty in the strict and formal sense. A house call from the doctor was understood as an act of utmost generosity, care, and concern for the patient. Requests for the doctor's house call were made only when the sick person appeared to be in danger.

The understanding of Christ as the divine physician is rooted in what can be called a healing soteriololgy. We are saved by the healing balm of Christ, Son and Word, and by the unction of the Spirit in which we are anointed. But if Christ's descent is given the attention it deserves, not only can it be said that Christ is the medicine of the soul, but we can also say that in Christ's descent God makes house calls. God's generous descent reaches out to the deepest level of human pain, anguish, and darkness—in our dying, our death—bearing balm that enlightens, enlivens, guides, and heals beyond our hope—even in the place of the dead.

A related image from the medical field may help here. Vaccine may serve as metaphor for the Spirit's way of healing by turning the very thing that kills us into the medicine that heals us, like the bronze serpent that Moses raised up in the desert to heal the Israelites of the fatal snake bites. Just as a vaccine introduces a version of the pathogen into a body in order to inoculate it, so are we healed and strengthened precisely by accepting, coming to terms with, and integrating the very thing that's killing us. Christ has shared our hell so that we do not suffer it alone. There is consolation in knowing that Christ has shared in our dying, in our death. And there is hope for us because he himself has been delivered from the hands of Hades. Christ is a vaccine in that he enters fully into the human experience of dying and death. In so doing he conquers our death and exchanges our perishability for imperishability. Confinement in the realm of dead bones is traded for living in the immensity of the ocean of God's love.

WAITING

Just as the gravely ill patient waits for the doctor's house call, we too must learn how to wait patiently. Just as there was no rushing the doctor who would be making house calls, so too the sick of soul must wait for the healing balm to penetrate deep down to the lowest, most unsightly regions of our hearts. These places are beyond our reach. Only the balm that Christ brings can extend through the cracks, the chinks in our armor.

But God's reach cannot be coaxed, let alone forced. Waiting, then, is a crucial dimension of living a spiritualty of Christ's descent.

Both Testaments bespeak the central place of waiting. The conclusion of the story of Jesus in the New Testament is a word of waiting. And waiting is how the narrative opens, as the central figures in his coming in flesh all wait in different ways. There is waiting at the beginning and waiting at the end.

In the various accounts of Christ's birth we find people who wait in different ways, and for different things. Consider the innkeeper who waits for business, then shuts out strangers because he has what he was waiting for: plenty of customers. He has no more room. He is not open; his door is shut.

Then there is Herod. His waiting is marked by fear or resentment. And so he is unable to be open to the message of the Magi. Fearful and anxious about losing power, his heart is insulated against what he might hear or see that would threaten the power he has. He waits in an attitude of suspicion, anxious that someone will come and take his power away from him.

The shepherds wait. Tradition has it that the shepherds were poor and simple people. They did not have great ambition. They had to struggle with life's demands, trusting that ordinary things would come their way, waiting for the fruits of their labor so that they could meet their daily needs. They wait in quiet trust. Theirs is a calm and restful waiting as they quietly tend to their duties on the hillsides. They are ready to hear. Their hearts are open to God's coming. Upon first hearing the startling news, they are surely frightened. But, because of their simplicity and their hope born in waiting, they waste no time in getting to the manger. They are able to surrender to what they have heard, and to what they see.

Mary waits with trust and openness to know God's will for her. She is attentive, expectant, waiting joyfully for the birth of her child. Her waiting is now coming to fullness. In spite of the fact that her circumstances are less than ideal, her waiting blossoms into a fullness that gives birth to the world's hope.

Joseph waits too. His waiting is one of attentiveness to the will of God, alert to the new responsibilities that will be his with the birth of the child. Because of his openness to what God is asking, he can surrender in waiting to what awaits him. He can live through his waiting with a heart open to whatever God asks of him. He is quietly present to God. He waits for the will of God in patience, open to learning how to care for and to protect this woman and the mysterious child.

What are our hearts waiting for? How are our hearts waiting? If we are honest with ourselves about what we are waiting for, then we will know how to wait. What is more, we will know how long to wait. For, if what we are waiting for is truly good and worthwhile, we will be willing to wait as long as it takes.

But the deeper question is: What is the one thing—which is not a thing at all—worth waiting for? We await the gift of the God who is with us in all our joys and hopes, but just as much in our grief and anguish. This is Emmanuel—God with us—in the tragedies of our lives just as much as in our triumphs.

We have to surrender to the waiting. It is in the waiting that we see what is truly worth waiting for: Love that comes to us in powerlessness and littleness, in death and generous descent without defense or force. And so we must wait quietly for and attentively to God's constant coming, more often than not in unexpected, startlingly gentle ways.

But the waiting is not all on our part. God waits in patience for us to accept the offer of love given and giving in the incarnation, death, and descent.

At times it seems that there is nothing worse than waiting. How we wait depends on what we are waiting for. Waiting for a long awaited trip abroad can be a delight. We thrill as the days pass and we ready ourselves for our departure. We say that getting there is half the fun. But it is different when we wait for the results of medical tests. This can be the most excruciating kind of waiting. Our lives seem "on hold" as we wait and wait and wait for some news. We wait for the elevator, in the checkout line at the supermarket, at the red light that just will not turn green fast enough. These days we are aggravated if we have to wait while our computer boots up. We wait for the birth of a child or grandchild. Nine months can seem like an eternity. We wait for an important phone call that never seems to come. Sometimes we wait for the many stresses and hassles and headaches of our busy lives to be over and done. Then, we think, we can get back some sense of balance and harmony, regain a small dose of tranquility amidst the crush of appointments and commitments, the flurry of activities that we busy ourselves with so as to ease the dis-ease of waiting.

Painful as it is, waiting is the soil in which hope is born. Waiting is that wide-open space of longing, of anticipation, of expectancy. It is when we long and anticipate and expect that hope may be born in us. Hope is openness to a future possibility that comes only as a gift—to those who know how to wait. In the waiting we attend to the wordless longing that endures at the heart of each of us. We wait so that something not of our own doing, not of our own making, can come into being.

PONDERING

Waiting provides the opportunity to ponder, to ponder long and lovingly. It is the call of the Holy Saturday people to ponder the magnitude of God's love in flesh amidst the pain we bear: our own, that of others, and that of the earth. If hoping is openness to what comes as a gift, pondering involves the quiet strength to carry the tension that is part of our life here and now, with all its pain and possibility. We must carry the tension of uncertainty, of not knowing exactly how things will work out, leaning on God's grace as we struggle each day in hope, seeing all around us so many reasons to give up and give in.

To ponder in the rich biblical sense does not mean reflecting on abstract concepts, or probing deep Greek philosophical thoughts. Pondering conveys, rather, a sense of mulling over, of considering, of weighing, of trying to balance things that seem to be at odds with one another, irreconcilable, yet willingly holding them in tension. By carrying the tension in a graceful and grace-laden heart, transformation can take place. Pondering gestates new life.

In the midst of our own very real pain and suffering, if we ponder in humility, with gentleness and patience, something does come to life that is not of our own making. By gracefully bearing it all, the tension is transformed, so that the pain and the hurt and the insult and the harm we bear is not given back in kind. Forgiveness is the return for insult; mercy, the reply to the hardened heart; a tranquil heart, the best response to the bloodthirsty and violent tongue. We are to hold in tension the misunderstanding and insult and ingratitude, waiting in hope until it all gestates into a living breathing manifestation of God's love—in and through us.

By his death and resurrection Jesus, Son and Word of the Father, has redeemed the world. But we will not soon be rid of the horror and pain of this world. These we must carry, even as we begin once again to sing a new song of God's goodness and fidelity. But in carrying these forward, our new song will ring out from deeper wells of compassion, echoing the empathy that comes only from profound suffering. We will come to a fresh understanding of what it means to follow the One Who is Love Born to be Crucified, and of what it means to live anew from the deepest hope for a new life wherein the power of love prevails over all evil.

We cannot erase what has been. We must bear it, carry it, so that something new can come to be. But what will come is not so much our doing. It is, rather, the gift of God whose love touches us at our most vulnerable point. What we await is Love's constant coming, coming to us in the regions of our deepest wound, making of it a region of wisdom. In wisdom we wait, carrying the tension that at times seems impossible to bear, looking for the coming of the new, for the gift that has been promised by the one who, on Saturday, lay in the tomb.

Even in such darkness we live with all the joy a heart can hold, a heart branded by pain and suffering yet transformed through pondering long and lovingly, so that the hope by which the whole church lives will not be extinguished.

In the cold and the dark of our hearts, amidst the terrors and trials, sometimes of our own making, something new is coming into being. What is it? What is this life gestating in us? What will come of this suffering and pain? The pondering heart knows that it is our gift and task to cling to God alone in hope, open to what is possible, but what comes only as a gift.

OUT OF NOTHING

Somewhat surprisingly, this spirituality shaped by Christ's death and descent is one of generativity or, better, creativity. Creativity describes an act of turning new and imaginative ideas into reality. It is characterized by the ability to see the world in new ways, to find hidden patterns, to make connections between seemingly unrelated phenomena, and to generate solutions. To this one might add that generating solutions is not simply fixing problems, but passing on insight, indeed wisdom, for the flourishing of others.

Stories of the long and painful processes of creativity abound. We learn from the Genesis accounts of creation that it did not happen in a flash, but rather over the course of six days. Dare we imagine that God rested on the seventh day because the creative act was utterly exhausting?

After Truman Capote's six-year-long excruciating ordeal of gathering the information for and composing *In Cold Blood*, the completed novel was an instant success. But the author was never able to write again. Writer's block may be an excuse to not move forward with the task at hand. Or it may be a period, sometimes quite long, when words are marinating, when thoughts are simmering, when ideas are aborning.

Consider that only a quarter of the architect Antoni Gaudí's basilica, *Sagrada Familia* in Barcelona, was finished at the time of his death in 1926. In the years since, by fits and starts, his vision is being realized. Only now, nearly a hundred years later, has the final stage of construction begun. A long gestation!

Georgia O'Keeffe began in the Midwest sketching with charcoal. Only later did she go bold: bright colors, broad strokes, flowers so big they overspilled and transcended her canvas. When macular degeneration clouded her vision, she could not continue to create the paintings for which she is now celebrated. But she did continue to paint in the dark. O'Keeffe is witness to the secret discipline that lies in the willingness to wait in the dark so that generativity, that life-giving energy, can bubble up from deep down cisterns.

It is into such darkness that the artist of any kind is plunged in the creative act, an act of generativity, the process of bringing something to life.

Whether it be the preparation of a wonderful meal for guests, a poetry reading before a small group, or the rehearsal for a solo before a discriminating audience, if the work is truly a creative act aimed at giving life to others, there is a measure of dread as we approach the task of preparation, both remote and immediate. Consider the artist sitting for hours or days in front of the canvas with palette in hand. She knows that she has something ahead of her, something that she has to do, indeed must do. But it just won't come. Until the time comes.

The creative act thus understood may be likened to the mother who experiences dread and fear, as well as hope, as her baby is passing through the birth canal. In the creative act of painting or building or composing or writing, it is as if a whole new world is lodged within me until in its own time it moves through my own birth canal.

The difference between the mother's baby passing through the birth canal and the activity of creating, or of generating life through art, music, building, painting, or writing, is that in these latter, there is a deep awareness that something has come from nothing.

While it is true that one must be disciplined and rigorous in the practice of one's art, when the work comes to light one often wonders from whence it has come. How did it come to be? I have put my whole soul into this, but it is not I who have done it. Indeed, it is as if something has come from nothing: from my own emptiness, lack of insight, irregular discipline, and failed efforts all along the way.

In the often excruciating, agonizing, creative, and generative act, it is as if I am pulling something from nothing. From nowhere. Something alive emerges from the deepmost regions of myself, so bottomless that it is both beneath and beyond my own being.

The mystery of Christ's descent discloses that it is from our own emptiness, out of the barren soil of our soul, from the dry fleshless bones and the shadowy shades of ourselves, that the love of God in Christ reaches so deep and yet deeper still finding and then pulling something from our nothing.

Living in the spirit of the Saturday we now know that God lives in and beyond death. Beyond death there is still God, creating and resurrecting. Beyond the void, out of nothing, comes something new, not of our doing. But we must learn to wait long and lovingly. Alone. In silence.

CHAPTER 10

Praying on the Saturday

ON MY ARRIVAL AT THE MONASTERY for Holy Week, one of the monks greeted me warmly: "Looks like you will be here for Hyacinth's funeral." Brother Hyacinth, a Trappist monk of many years, was in the infirmary dying. He had been dying for days. Of sturdy stock from Detroit, Hyacinth never missed a day of work, was never absent from his place at prayer and Mass. He was one of the few of the older Trappists who remembered all of their sign language from when they observed strict silence. And he taught me. What I remember best is the sign for "Break for black coffee!"

The brothers tended Hyacinth carefully in his last days. As his time drew near, he simply would not go. Early one morning the abbot went to the dying monk's bedside to assure him that Jesus was coming soon. "Jesus is coming soon." "Jesus is coming soon." Over and over again. With hardly an ounce of strength or breath, Hyacinth looked squarely at the abbot: "You have to know how to wait."

Years earlier I visited the same monastery to give conferences to the monks. On that occasion I had the chance to take a walk with an abbot who was making his retreat at the monastery. He had just stepped aside after having served as abbot of the largest Trappist monastery in the United States for more than a quarter of a century. He was making a retreat to try to discern what his next step in life might be.

I asked him what had been his single most important contribution, and then his biggest shortcoming as abbot. It took him a while to answer. But he did. Quietly.

Why stop here, I thought. So I put the more important question to him. "After so many years in monastic life, what have you learned about God?" His immediate response: "No one has ever asked me that question." Pause; long pause; painfully long pause. "I suppose I have learned about the silence of God."

Each day monks rise at three in the morning to begin a day of prayer and work. Seven times throughout the day the monks gather together in the abbey church to pray: psalms, hymns, scripture, readings from the Fathers of the Church, prayers of praise and supplication. In addition to this there is the Eucharist each day. Apart from this there is manual labor. And there is very little distraction or entertainment. After a lifetime of such deep and disciplined work and prayer over the course of almost half a century: "The silence of God."

Waiting. Silence. Alone. Praying into the Dark.
The hardest thing about being in the dark is not being able to see. Whenever we find ourselves in a place of deep anxiety, doubt, or fear, we can't seem to tell down from up, left from right. When we're plunged into that kind of darkness, we don't even know what's true, or if anything means anything.

From these depths we are summoned to look forward, to hope, to give account of the hope that is within us for ourselves and for the world.

It is in these infernal circles, both personal and communal, that we can find luminous traces of God. We strain to hear God's voice. But there is only the silence. In that silence we see in Christ's dead body the stirrings of the love that survives death.

Even here, in the circles of suffering and hell, we can place our trust in God's Word, and there find the words of deep lament. Here we name before God what is not right, what is evil, what should not be. We dare to name the negative. We boldly express to God our disappointment, our desolation, our anger in the face of the truth of things as they are, and never seem to change. But this is the God who is our God even when we seem to be left for lost—like the One who cried out loud to the heavens but was left to die a failure

He made passage to be present to humanity through his own abasement, unto death, to the dead, into hell. Those who put their trust in him will make passage with him to the Father, emptied out in him and in the Spirit. Yet even as we praise and thank God for the new life that is yet to come, we sense in the pit of our stomach a sense of horror that cannot be denied: How long, O Lord?

In those hellish places and spaces and conditions we listen for the voice of the Father calling us to life again. But there is only the silence.

The deepest kind of prayer is known in being seized in wonder: at the shimmering beauty of God's Word in flesh, in wondering "Why?" as expressed in Jesus' cry from the cross in abandonment.

We are branded by such sickness of soul that our prayer, fumbling to find words, can only rise up from the depths, from the bottoms. It is from the lowest rung, the shaky foothold on which he took his place, that we can look upon Christ or call God "Father": from within the circles of hellish suffering.

Out of the depths I cried. I wondered: Why? *Silence*. And from there beheld the One crucified, dead, interred, descended, and so stand now in wonder at the shimmering traces of God's love that can be known in his body still bearing wounds.

This day we are passing through the circles of hell, led by the Christ who first made passage. As Christ was interred and descended to be among those who were in the absence of God, so it is in passing through the place of the dead that God is manifest, not as an immutable and almighty nameless being, but as the one who is Father and who has given the Son and the Spirit whose love knows no bounds.

It is the time of great silence

> How to face into the suffering of whole nations, races, classes—of whole peoples—and respond to the call to heal wounds, not just of individual persons, but of the earth and all the living?
>
> *Silence*.
>
> What of the integration of sexual desire in a culture obsessed with the beauty of the human body?
>
> *Silence*.
>
> How to address the need for the proper disposition and distribution of material goods in a world whose

economic engines are near exhaustion, indeed on the verge of complete collapse, yet still manage to drive millions into the squalor that breeds disease and fuels violence?

Silence.

What of the need for forgiveness and reconciliation, a "purification of memories" to which John Paul II called the whole church?

Silence.

How to speak rightly of the justice of God, even while recognizing that we ourselves are part of systems of sin?

Silence.

How to ask pardon for my own part in the systemic evil infecting both society and church?

Silence.

What is my part in bringing about the kingdom, working quietly toward the reordering of the world now and to come in the order of divine justice?

Silence.

Out of the depths, I cry to you.
Come. Deliver us.

Silence.

In the silence, in the emptiness of the Saturday, God does not speak. At other times God speaks. And then God does not speak. And then God may speak again. Saturday is *the* moment of non-speaking, of non-saying. One of the hardest lessons to learn in the spiritual life is this: When there is nothing to say, you say nothing. On the Saturday there is nothing to be said. And there is no saying. There is only the silence.

There is a night of utter solitude where no one can reach us. There is a door through which we must pass completely alone. In dying and death we are utterly alone. The loneliness where love cannot reach is hell. Yet God in Christ reaches through and beyond our ultimate loneliness, down into the depths of our abandonment. He is there where and when we cannot be reached any longer.

Silence, the sound I've never heard.

I'll stand here and gaze upon—into—it.

Stretching into the silence, there is nothing to fear,
for when there is nothing,
there is only God.

Suggestions for Further Reading

Chapter 2

There are numerous sources that offer a fuller explanation of how some Asian and Southeast Asian peoples understand death and those who have died. A popular articulation is found in Việt Thành Nguyễn's short story, "Black-Eyed Women," in *The Refugees*, pp. 1–21. New York: Grove Press, 2017.

Chapter 3

For the view of *kenosis*, descent, and Holy Saturday that undergirds the present volume, see Hans Urs von Balthasar, *Mysterium Paschale: The Mystery of Easter*. Grand Rapids, MI: Eerdmans, 1993.

For an understanding of the Syriac tradition on the descent and ongoing *kenosis*, see Irina Kukota, "Christ, the Medicine of Life: The Syriac Fathers on the Lord's Descent into Hell." *Road to Emmaus* 6, no. 1 (Winter 2005): 17–56.

For a further reflection on the Trinity that complements this present work, see Michael Downey, *Altogether Gift: A Trinitarian Spirituality*. Maryknoll, NY: Orbis Books, 2000.

For more on the historical Jesus, see John Meier, *A Marginal Jew: Rethinking the Historical Jesus*. Five volumes. See especially volume one. New Haven, CT: Yale University Press, 1991.

For an excellent treatment of the emergence of the creedal affirmation of Christ's descent and the early development of the *descensus* clause, to which the present volume is greatly indebted, see Martin Connell, "*Descensus Christi ad Inferos*: Christ's Descent to the Dead." *Theological Studies* 62 (2001): 262–82.

Chapter 4

For inspiring insights regarding a spirituality rooted in the mystery of Holy Saturday, see Alan E. Lewis, *Between Cross and Resurrection: A Theology of Holy Saturday*. Grand Rapids, MI: Eerdmans, 2001.

For further examination of the contrast between Jesus' "descent to the dead" and his "descent into hell," see Martin Connell, "*Descensus Christi ad Inferos*: Christ's Descent to the Dead." *Theological Studies* 62 (2001): 262–82.

Chapter 5

For Jürgen Moltmann on the God who risks suffering by being self-giving love, see his *The Crucified God: The Cross of Christ as the Foundation and Criticism of Christian Theology*. Minneapolis, MN: Fortress, 1994.

Chapter 6

For more on Pope Francis' understanding of "existential peripheries," see Jorge Mario Bergoglio's address to his brother cardinals on the eve of his election to the Chair of Peter on March 13, 2013.

For a reliable treatment of intermediate states of life after death, see Peter C. Phan, *Living into Death, Dying into Life: A Christian Theology of Death and Eternal Life*. Hobe Sound, FL: Lectio Publishing, 2014.

Chapter 7

For Karl Rahner on hope, see his "On the Theology of Hope," *Theological Investigations* X, chap. 13, pp. 242–59. New York: Herder and Herder, 1973.

For a nuanced reading of Thomas Aquinas on the matter of the cessation of hope at death, see the comments on purgatory in his *Respondeo* to article 2 of question 2 of the first appendix of the Supplement to the *Tertia Pars* of the *Summa Theologica*. On the *res* of the Eucharist, see his *Commentary on Book IV of the Sentences*, d.12, q.2, a.11.

Chapter 8

For deeper insight into Hans Urs von Balthasar's understanding of the Paschal Mystery, see his *Mysterium Paschale: The Mystery of Easter*. Grand Rapids, MI: Eerdmans, 1993.

Chapter 9

For more on the movement inspired by Francis and Clare of Assisi, see Regis J. Armstrong, William J. Short, J. A. Wayne Hellman, *Francis of Assisi: Early Documents*, three volumes, and Regis J. Armstrong, *Clare of Assisi: Early Documents*, both published by New City Press, Hyde Park, NY.

For an overview of the Focolare Movement and spirituality, see *Chiara Lubich: Essential Writings*. Hyde Park, NY: New City Press, 2007.

For insights into Dominican spirituality, see Simon Tugwell, *Early Dominicans: Selected Writings*. New York/Mahwah, NJ: Paulist Press, 1982.

For insights into the spirituality of Jean Vanier and l'Arche, see Jean Vanier, *Becoming Human*. New York/Mahwah, NJ: Paulist Press, 1998.